Rowdy Entrepreneurs and Insecure Dinosaurs:

Popular Strategies for Innovation After the End of Endings

Rowdy Entrepreneurs and Insecure Dinosaurs:

Popular Strategies for Innovation
After the End of Endings

Murat Karamuftuoglu

Winchester, UK
Washington, USA

First published by Zero Books, 2013
Zero Books is an imprint of John Hunt Publishing Ltd., Laurel House, Station Approach,
Alresford, Hants, SO24 9JH, UK
office1@jhpbooks.net
www.johnhuntpublishing.com
www.zero-books.net

For distributor details and how to order please visit the 'Ordering' section on our website.

ISBN: 978 1 78099 287 7

A CIP catalogue record for this book is available from the British Library.

Design: Stuart Davies

Printed and bound by CPI Group (UK) Ltd, Croydon, CR0 4YY

We operate a distinctive and ethical publishing philosophy in all
areas of our business, from our global network of authors to
production and worldwide distribution.

CONTENTS

Preface: This is Insane, or Minding the Small Print[1]

What is insane? And what is the 'listening suggestion' that lurks behind the very first endnote of the book? The latter is a bit easier to answer, so let me start with it. Every book has a story to tell but not a song to hum to. Well, this book has – in fact, not one but several (on the last count it was fifteen, enough to fill a CD album, or in the old days a double LP). However, don't count yourself lucky, thinking that 'if the ideas are not good I can at least listen the songs' (which, I assure you, are good). You need a computer with an internet connection, or better, a record player, now back in fashion after surviving the onslaught of the CD and more lately MP3 formats, if you want to hear any of them. Neither the music nor the lyrics of the songs are included in the book (more on this below). Nor is this a book on music.

The book rather aims to shed a new light on the process of *innovation*, more specifically on the role of body and mind, the everyday and the ordinary in innovation. It has a philosophical and political outlook, and entertains both micro and macro level analyses. To my knowledge, it is the first book of its kind that mingles *popular culture* theory (as well as politics and philosophy) with innovation and entrepreneurship. It is written, true to the spirit of popular culture, in a lively style (you see, I have been an academic so far, this was my chance to escape the dryness of academic prose) with abundant popular cultural references, and textual and visual puns, hence, the references to popular music in the endnotes.

Songs (references to the titles) are not added in any systematic way to the text. I have not sat down and thought which song might be more fun, relevant, etc., to listen to while reading this or that section. For whatever reason I am not quite sure, the ones in the footnotes are the first ones that pop up in my mind – more or less by free association (but please do not attempt to psychoanalyze me on the basis of the suggested playlist, as there are many other favorite bands and songs which I withheld!).

How about the insanity and the small print mentioned above? It refers to the insanity of holding on to the old copyright laws in the face of increasing ease of use of information with the advances in digital technologies, in particular, the World Wide Web. With the ease with which one can copy, modify, adapt and use another's work it is hard to enforce the old laws on the Web (remember the failure of the recent attempt in the U.S. to legislate the old regime on the online world, known as Stop Online Piracy Act or SOPA). Information wants to be free, and is indeed becoming freer, although not in the print world. Despite the fact that on the Web it is practically impossible to enforce the old copyright regime, when it comes to the print form, judges and the lawyers hold on to their old guns.

The book in your hands is not the 'author's cut'. The original author's version, which has been seen only by a handful of friends, included the lyrics of the songs referenced in this edition, as well as many other photographs. The only images that are remaining in this edition are those from *Wikimedia Commons*, which is a user-created online repository of free-use images, or the works of my personal friends, except the one from an artist who kindly gave permission to use one of his works pro-bono. Thank you Phil Ross for your inspiring work (see Chapter 4) and the kind permission to use it here. My thanks also go to Cem and Seda who have kindly provided four of the photographs you will enjoy in the book. And thank you Wikimedia Commons for the rest of the images in the book.

Anything more would have required going through the process of individually contacting artists or their agents, representatives, etc., to license each photograph or the lyric separately, and a considerable sum of cash. In many cases it was not even possible to track the copyright owner of a photograph replicated in countless Web pages (but this does not ensure that you will be free of the threat of court action if you use them in your book). In the case of the lyrics, it would involve identifying the publishing house that owns the copyright and negotiating a license, usually for a substantial fee. The only lyric to be found in this book is a short excerpt from the Toreador Song from the opera *Carmen*, which is in the public domain due to its old age.

I am not advocating free use (as in 'free beer') of artists' creations. They should definitely be compensated for their work, however the current intellectual property system hinders greater use of artists' output by smaller publishers, or first-time authors, whose books may or may not sell a few thousand copies. There are many proposals for compensating the artists in the digital age while maintaining a free-for-all system for artworks and music. One such proposal is to impose a levy on internet service and/or Telecom providers to fund new content creation, similar to the levy imposed on recordable media such as cassette tapes and CDs in many countries, known as the *private copying levy* or *tax*. Similarly, several proposals for distribution of royalties gathered in this way have been put forward, including those based on measures such as the number of downloads, usage, or direct internet voting. Obviously, each proposed scheme has its advantages and disadvantages and countless arguments and counter-arguments are made for each.

However, one thing is certain in my mind from my experience in writing my first book. The licensing process can substantially be made easier for all by simply centralizing the whole process. It is not hard to imagine a centralized Web-based worldwide registry of content where content owners register their work and users register the amount of their use. It would also be helpful if the licensing fees are made payable only if a certain number of the copies of the book are sold or a certain amount of revenue is generated from sales. This would be a more fruitful arrangement for both the content creators and users as books that are geared towards general readership and priced accordingly tend to avoid use of any material that requires upfront payment given that most books published in that segment make a loss. I am sure that many counter-arguments can be leveled against such a proposal, but one thing is certain that the current system needs fixing, and almost anything would be better than what we have got presently.

Electronic books or eBooks pose other challenges. Different screen sizes of various readers and tablets available on the market mean that unless the book is designed and laid out separately for all devices, which is economically not feasible for most publishers (especially not in these times), it is impossible to guarantee that images and other formatting will appear as intended or the captions stay together with their accompanying pictures, figures, or tables. I apologize, therefore, if the eBook in your hand suffers from such problems.

Peer-to-peer file sharing, free software, and user-generated content are the frontiers where the old economic system is bursting at its seams. The ongoing worldwide economic crisis that started with the 2008 financial meltdown is a telltale sign that the current world order will be unlikely to hold its own for very long. One of the reviewers of an early draft of this book commented that my reference to the 'credit crunch' of 2008 could become obsolete by the time the book is published; therefore, it is better removed. That was more than two years ago. My response was that you shouldn't worry (or rather you should worry) about that: this is not one of those relatively short periods of recession that follow periods of rapid economic growth. The current crises cannot either be explained, in my view, by Kondratiev waves – long cycles (forty to sixty years) of boom followed by depression that characterize the modern capitalist world economy first identified by Nikolai Dmitriyevich Kondratiev (1892-1938), and popularized by Joseph Alois Schumpeter (1883-1950), the founding father of innovation and entrepreneurship studies. Kondratiev and Schumpeter showed that one possible explanation of long-term cycles of 'creative destruction' is major technological changes or 'great innovations' as in the shift from 'The Age of Oil, Electricity, the Automobile and Mass Production' ca. 1908 to 'The Age of Information and Telecommunications' ca. 1971. There is, I believe, a more fundamental ongoing change that underlies the continuing economic troubles, which will not be resolved until we move from the current unipolar Atlantic-dominated world order to a new multipolar world where the Pacific basin will become the center of economic and political power – a theme explored in the final chapter of the book. The reader could, therefore, rightfully expect to find references to popular songs in Chinese, Hindi and Russian in the future editions of the book!

What will come next to replace the current world socio-economic system may not be what I hoped for or dreamt of while writing this book. I like to think of the system that will one day, no doubt in my mind, come to existence as a *community of friends* who are blessed (or perhaps, 'condemned') with the freedom to 'invent' their own meanings relevant to their everyday lives, bottom-up from their own authentic experiences, not only on the online world but also in the physical world made up of flesh and bodily juices. Such a community would prize creativity and creation of new meanings out of everyday experiences instead of accepting ready-made ones that are pushed top-down by the 'culture industry' – a term coined by the critical theorists Theodor Adorno (1903-1969) and Max Horkheimer (1895-1973).

I would think that the happiest period of my life was from my late teenage years to my late twenties. What distinguished that decade from my later 'adult' life were the intensities and passions around which we, with my friends, collectively constructed our everyday lives. The common interests, dreams, and passions we discovered and explored, endless conversations we entertained, the fun we had with no or little money, the 'reality' that we invented – part out of fiction, part out of our concrete daily mundane experiences – that made our existence a little more meaningful. It was a period where there were no real foes as Friedrich Nietzsche (1844-1900), the (in)famous nineteenth century philosopher – who became insane towards the end of his life – wrote in response to the Ancient Greek philosopher Aristotle's statement about friendship:

> And so, we can endure ourself, let us also endure other people; and perhaps to each of us there will come the more joyful hour when we exclaim:
> 'Friends, there are no friends!' thus said the dying sage;
> 'Foes, there are no foes!' say I, the living fool.[2]

Apart from the people already mentioned above, there are many others who directly or indirectly, or by their mere existence contributed to this work, including those friends of mine who have not given feedback on the drafts I sent to them, and those I have never met in person. Thank you Öymen, Olga, Jonathan, Ali, Kaan, Aydemir, Ömer, Andreas, Gonca and all members of 'Akdeniz/Bahçeli' mailing list, and all artists, musicians, poets and philosophers I have cited (and not) in this book. Thank you, especially, my little friend Leonardo Kaya. My thanks are also due to my publisher and the editorial team at Zero Books. Thank you Carol Givner for your helpful critique on the first draft of the book. And last but not least, I thank Ercan for his enduring and unfailing friendship since the age of two or three.

London, July 2012

Of Passions, Skills, Innovation and New Economy

• Innovation and New Economy • A Bit of a Sci-Fi • Of Hearts and Bones • One-Trick Pony • Afterlife • A Riddle: Skulls and Vats, Skyscrapers and Telescopes • Quantity Drives Quality Out Everywhere

Innovation and New Economy

This little book is about innovation, specifically innovation in the context of postmodern society and postmodern information economy. Postmodernity is characterized in the economic realm with the rise of information as an economic commodity in addition to the three fundamental pillars of traditional economies; namely, money, human labor, and raw materials. Informational economies are marked by the displacement, to a considerable extent, of industrial production by finance and service sectors of the economy.

Disembodied information, that is, information extracted from real, material contexts and represented as digits in computers and circulated around the globe at the speed of light in digital communication networks is conferred with almost magical powers in the current economic and political discourse of globalism. All reality according to the dominant postmodern discourse is made up of language, representation and information, which can be manipulated, transformed as one wishes, and refracted through the glass screen of telecommunication media before projected back onto the reality to replace it. 'More real than real' is the reality of the 'hyperreality' created by modern information and communication technologies in the famous words of media theorist Jean Baudrillard[3] whose analysis of the postmodern media world came to replace the older theories of the bygone TV age of Marshall McLuhan, of 'medium is the message' fame.[4]

According to postmodern theorists we need nothing more than language and information; we *are* indeed language and information. Life is made of information. Invention and innovation are thus reduced to language games and combinations at will of disembodied and decontextualized information relieved from all chains that hold it hostage to material reality.

This book argues to the contrary: we cannot innovate by 'thinking' alone. Invention and innovation are not only a matter of language games or information logics; it is more a matter of material activities and practices. We are not disembodied ether-like creatures. We live and inhabit a material world within which all inventions and innovations take place. This book is set to trace the circulation of people and artifacts, ideas and passions, around the globe, a process that brings about happy inventions and innovations. Chapter 2 is devoted specifically to the historical account of this process from the birth of the first modern ideas in the East to the dawn of the Age of Discovery in the West.

The central argument of the book is that joyful, skilled, playful activities and practices are the basis of most, if not all, inventions and innovations. This perspective puts the practice of everyday life at the heart of invention and innovation. Chapter 3 investigates the strategies of invention and innovation of some of the big names and companies, specifically, Virgin, Microsoft, and Apple that are much loved or abhorred today. The discussion in this chapter highlights the similarities between the way everyday culture and life are produced and the practices that produce popular inventions and innovations.

Chapter 4 continues this line of investigation by looking at the new forms of art and science experiments that have become popular in recent years. The emerging hybrid works of 'artscience' or 'information arts' that give physical shape to information highlight the importance of skilled, passionate, embodied, material, and practical work in innovation.

Just as ordinary everyday life is the basis of many of the most useful and popular inventions and innovations, it is also the basis of the whole economy. The other main argument of this book is that ordinary people and ordinary everyday life – with all its repetitions, passionate amplifications of small differences, and creativity – produces the real economy, and as such 'popular economy', more than 'political economy' reduced to productivity measures, should be at the heart of economics and economic policies.

Chapter 5 puts innovation in the context of the general economy, and speculates about the new forms economic relations could take in the future popular economy of the people. The chapter concludes by arguing along the lines of the not-very-well-known but increasingly relevant French sociologist Gabriel Tarde (1843-1904), that economics of innovation and the economy at large should be understood as 'the science of passionate interests' of people.

A Bit of a Sci-fi

What would be life like, after the end of all ends, when we fly past all posts: post-modernity, post-humanity, post-everything in a rush? Can we exist without our bodies in a post-human age to come? Is it possible for the brain to live in a vacuum? More importantly for our purposes here, can we keep invent and innovate by our brains alone? For the excessively reductionist philosophy of science of the twenty-first century, the brain in a vat, virtual existence without an anchor in the material world, seems to be a possible scenario. I will argue, however, for the impossibility of it: we cannot exist or sustain with our minds alone, let alone invent and innovate. Our capacity to act on the external world, to change the world, to innovate, depends on bodies as *afferent* and *efferent*, sensory and motor, sites of interaction with the material world. We are not only abstract calculating or theorizing machines; we also are sensual beings.

Nevertheless, lets indulge in a bit of a sci-fi fantasy of out-of-body virtual existence expounded by Hilary Putnam (1926-), a contemporary American philosopher:

Here is a science fiction possibility discussed by philosophers: Imagine that a human being (you can imagine this to be yourself) has been subjected to an operation by an evil scientist. The person's brain (your brain) has been removed from the body and placed in a vat of nutrients, which keeps the brain alive. The nerve endings have been connected to a super-scientific computer, which causes the person whose brain it is to have the illusion that everything is perfectly normal. There seem to be people, objects, the sky, etc.; but really, all the person (you) is experiencing is the result of electronic impulses travelling from the computer to the nerve endings. The computer is so clever that if the person tries to raise his hand, the feedback from the computer will cause him to 'see' and 'feel' the hand being raised. Moreover, by varying the program, the evil scientist can cause the victim to 'experience' (or hallucinate) any situation or environment the evil scientist wishes.[5]

Is this a plausible scenario for our future? This and similar thought experiments, from the time of Descartes to the present, have puzzled and continue to puzzle countless generations of philosophers and scientists. But, I think, it is the wrong sort of question. Wrong questions attract wrong answers. This is the sort of mistake that causes what renegade philosopher Wittgenstein calls 'mental cramps' and 'philosophical torments'.

For me, the question is not whether the 'brain in a vat' could actually know it is in a vat or not, but what would happen when the plug is pulled off from the wall? What would happen when

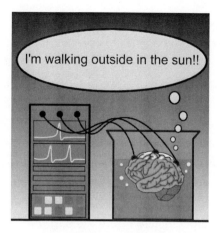

Source: Wikimedia Commons
(http://commons.wikimedia.org/wiki/File%3ABrain_in_a_vat_(en).png)

the skills we humans have accumulated throughout many millennia of our evolution have been made redundant suddenly? What would life on earth be like when large portions of the population have been incapacitated for work as a result of deskilling? What would the end of the story be like when everybody becomes a 'sales consultant' (!) or 'retail representative' (!) in a fast food chain so much so that nobody remembers any more how to cook pasta at home?

Of Hearts and Bones[6]

What would remain of the brain in the vat when the power is turned off? A stockpile of compost? Precisely!! And, reassuringly so! This is how organic life is renewed on this planet called the earth: one man's dung is another man's manure! Every ending not only has a beginning, but it is a beginning of a new beginning. A useful trope that will guide our discussions in this book.

There is, however, another side to the brain in a vat. We all are in reality a bit like that, that is, brains in a vat, or more to the point, biological computing machines that crunch symbols, symbolic representations of the world. We are, in part, 'theorizing machines'; constantly contemplating the world. The soft machine in our skull constantly bothers us with theories of what the world is and how it should be. But, we have also got in our bodies little bone machines and heart machines; we not only think but also sense, feel and affect. We not only theorize about the world but also change it by acting on it. We are also made of passions, dreams, habits, and learned skills. Our hearts and bones are repositories of 'passionate interests', to use the words of long-forgotten sociologist Gabriel Tarde, of integrated skills and artisanal competencies. While the soft machine seems to be the throne of rational and theoretical knowledge, the bone machines and heart machines are where our passions and manual virtuosities are treasured.

One-Trick Pony[7]

The conundrum we are facing, as the human race, is the following: the 'organic composition' of our economies, and our culture and arts, in short our lives, have been constantly decreasing for a long time. Organic composition of capital is a term in political economy that denotes the ratio between constant capital (all means of production, such as plants and machinery, land and buildings) and variable capital (human power).

True, capitalism is a beast! A particular beast indeed! A one-trick pony is what it really is for the most part. It ticks mainly by extracting surplus value by reducing the cost associated with the human labor in the production process. In other words, while the contribution of the human element decreases in production of goods, the mechanical element increases; a strategy which has become particularly conspicuous with the advances made in Information and Communication Technologies and factory automation from the second half of the twentieth century onwards. If capitalism had to choose one science to keep for itself that would be computer science for this reason. While the weight of the living bodies disappears in the production process, the weight of the dead machines increases. This is the basic formula of capitalism.

Afterlife[8]

However, there is a small problem! The decrease in the organic composition of capital[9] cannot be maintained indefinitely! In other words, production cannot be totally free of human element, as total automation of production would not yield any surplus value or profits. Why? Simple: while productivity increases with the decrease in the organic composition, average profit per unit of output also decreases as the purchasing power needed to buy them decreases on average. Remember that the human work force has just been made redundant; nobody is left to buy our precious goods!

This is the point of no return. Where to head when the plug is pulled off the wall, when the bone machine is broken and the heart machine is torn off? Where to head after the end of all ends?

There has been a lot of talk in recent years, and indeed throughout the known human history, of 'the ends'. Unlike our story of brain in a vat that turned to compost when its plug is unplugged, most religious eschatologies have happy endings, at least for the faithful and the virtuous. In such scenarios the end of the world is followed by the final judgment that leads to eternal bliss of non-change, of sameness. In heaven nothing really happens.

Outside of the religious, secular eschatologies have recently prophesized similar endings and beginnings. Most famously we have heard, but not actually seen, the end of History - or more aptly, 'His-story' – declared by Francis Fukuyama, American philosopher and political economist. Similarly, he promised a blissful coexistence of political powers after the downfall of the socialist world at the end of the 1980s, that is, at least until the next credit crunch! There are other similar secular eschatologies and prophecies, though usually with more ambivalent endings: 'the end of the art', 'the end of science', 'the death of author', to name but a few. The post-modernity, our present state of existence (or non-existence depending on your viewpoint), is literally littered by countless other cadavers.

Outside of the linear eschatologies of the Abrahamic religions, and their secular doppelgängers, there are cyclic eschatologies that promise the return of not very much of the same, but reincarnation with a difference. In such narratives, the binary opposition is played out not between life and death, but between death and rebirth; every death is followed by rebirth not elsewhere in afterlife but in another life here on this planet. I believe this is a more fruitful way of thinking of our future life on this planet, as well as our past; a theme that will be explored in Chapters 2 and 5.

A Riddle: Of Vats and Skulls, Skyscrapers and Telescopes[10]

If 'brain in a vat' is one metaphor that helps us understand our current state of affairs, the other is that of the skyscraper. Here is a little riddle: *What is common between a 'brain in a vat' and a skyscraper?* They both distort our view of reality!

As we mulled over earlier, the soft machine in our skull cogitates about the world and constructs ever-tall theories of what it is and how it should be. It, in fact, constructs a virtual reality, a science fiction, to immerse itself in. This virtual reality constructed part out of science and part out of fiction acts as the vat of nutrients that keeps the brain alive in the narrative of Putnam's 'brain in a vat'. We, humans, create virtual realities that make our existence in this unknown journey called life a little more meaningful. But, past a certain point, the harmless-looking fantasies of our minds create a smoke screen that blurs our vision. The process is not unlike that of building ever-taller skyscrapers. The theoretical knowledge that crowns the soft machine is like a skyscraper, in the sense that the taller it grows the further it takes us away from the ground that sustains us. As it grows taller and taller, the sight of the ground of reality on which it is built is lost. To reality check; bigger and bigger optical instruments that bring distant reality nearer are needed, that is until our perspective completely loses sight of the big picture. As we will see in the next chapter, an inevitable collapse ensues; the tall building imparts more weight than the real estate on which it is built can carry.

Photo courtesy of Cem Devecioğlu.

I call this Vertical Epistemic Development or VED, which is 'progress' to most people. The alternative route is to develop horizontally so as to cover more of the ground without losing the sight of reality. This route of development, which I call as Horizontal Ontic Development or HOD is the main theme of the last chapter of this book.

Science suffers from VED at first hand. The publish or perish ethos that infected much of academia in the last decades has made sure that too many inconsequential papers are published *and* perish, while acute social problems duck to dodge the telescopic views from the dizzying heights of theoretic skyscrapers.

Epistemology is the branch of philosophy that studies the nature of knowledge, its foundations, and its extent and validity. Here, 'Vertical Epistemic Development' simply means theoretical development with little or no concern for the underlying reality.

Ontology is the branch of philosophy that deals with the nature of being. Here, 'Horizontal Ontic Development' means the development of the 'real estate' (the sum of all natural, artificial, and human resources) on which the social life on this planet depends.

Quantity Drives Quality Out Everywhere

I will argue that wherever there is excessive VED, be it in economy, art, philosophy, science or technology, there is a decrease in quality at the expense of quantity, which degrades our artisanal competencies and debases our passions. The end result is a decrease in the overall quality of life for the whole planet.

In postmodern thought and philosophy VED manifests itself as endless play on words and babble, commentaries on commentaries, absolute relativism that removes any hope of meaningful debate, political correctness and politics of identity that avoid real socio-economic issues and problems.

The myopic problems that stem from VED are perhaps nowhere as acute or obvious as in postmodern economies. The implosion of the derivatives balloon in 2008 caused by the massive and unfounded expansion of credit under the regime of finance capitalism, made too obvious the level of our inebriation with science fictional economics that produces virtual wealth at the expense of the real. The real wealth is the wealth of a quality life based on an integrated, wholesome diet of cognitive and artisanal skills and competencies; a topic discussed throughout this book.

On the art side of the things, there is the post-Duchamp (or should I have said post-Saatchi) syndrome, the endless search for novelty for the sake of novelty and shock value (as well as fame and fortune). The petite shock tactics of most contemporary conceptual art could, however, hardly succeed in hiding the abyss of irrelevance that art has fallen into. As Ian Masslow,

Manneken Pis, Jerome Duquenoy, 1618
(Photo: Myrabella / Wikimedia Commons / CC-BY-SA-3.0,
http://commons.wikimedia.org/wiki/File%3ABruxelles_Manneken_Pis.jpg);
Fountain, Marcel Duchamp, 1917
(Photo: Micha L. Rieser / Wikimedia Commons / CC-BY-SA-3.0,
http://commons.wikimedia.org/wiki/File%3AFontaine-Duchamp.jpg).

then-chairman of the Institute of Contemporary Art in London put it, rather forcefully but perhaps tactlessly, most conceptual art has become 'pretentious, self-indulgent, craftless tat!'

The process that has driven skills and crafts out of artistic production is uncannily similar to the process of deskilling of workers at the end of the eighteenth century by a series of innovations in textile manufacturing technology that fired the industrial revolution. In particular, the advent of automation with the invention of the mechanical loom in 1801, also known as the 'Jacquard loom', tilted the balance between humans and machines in favor of the latter, and upset the chemistry of the 'organic composition' in production forever.

The idea behind both processes is based on the same trick: separation of intellect and body, mental skills and manual skills, that is, extraction of 'quality' from living bodies, and turning it into 'quantity' by means of mechanical processes. As today's artists could – and do – make music without playing a single instrument or note, or create art without getting their hands dirty in paint or charcoal, the mechanical loom made obsolete the skills of the artisan worker. Sure, the lost manual skills have been replaced by cognitive skills needed to design and maintain automatons. This is, however, exactly the point I want to make. Quality in life, quality life, depends on a harmonious balance between cognitive and artisanal skills. This is precisely what has been upset since the industrial revolution.

As a 'MIDI note' generated by a music synthesizer, which is basically a standardized representation – or more accurately, a dead replica of the qualities such a timber, pitch, and volume of live sound – never captures the warmth of live performance, or a machine woven carpet cannot replicate the beauty of hand-knotted Oriental kilims and rugs, mass produced goods miss the quality imparted by human hand to uniquely crafted things.

Quality is related to the living body's heightened sensitivity to discern meaningful distinctions between objects and substances, which is a prerequisite for creating something new. It is intimately tied to bodily affections and adrenalin-driven passions, that is, human aesthetic capacity. We invent and innovate, as will be shown in Chapter 3 and 4, chiefly by embodied, sensory interaction with other bodies and our environment.

This is why, as I will argue in this book, invention and innovation are primarily an ontic enterprise, that is, a practice of engaging with material reality, and changing the world with creative activity. It is only secondarily a cognitive or theoretical business. When this order is upset, lower quality imitation takes precedence, as it will be illustrated in Chapter 3.

The predominance of vertical epistemic development at the expense of horizontal ontic development in today's social, economic, and cultural life is at the heart of our current troubles and conundrums. The following juxtaposition of skyscrapers and 'Cloud Gate' – a public sculpture erected in the AT&T Plaza in Millennium Park Chicago by Indian-born British artist Anish Kapoor that reflects and distorts on its smooth skull-like metallic surface the city's skyline – brings together the two metaphors that best represent the state of desolation and distortion in today's economic and cultural life.

Composite photo courtesy of Seda Usubütün.

We are now set to take a short tour of the circulation of passions, skills, ideas, artifacts, and inventions, as well as peoples, around the globe, and en route the rise, fall and rebirth of empires and civilizations.

2

The Beginnings of the Ends:
A Short Archaeology

• Da Da Da: The End of Everything • ca. AD 610: End of
Prophethood • Age of Discovery • End of the Age of
Discovery: Deskilling and Plasticization • Circumnavigating
the Globe • Afro-Asiatic Age of Discovery • End of the
Muslim Age of Discovery • Collapsing New Buildings
• Lessons from the Ends of the World • The End of History:
Here Comes Hegel • Dialectics Old and New

Da Da Da: The End of Everything[11]

We live in the age of end of everything. Postmodernism, the sign
of our times that *tolled* the *death knell* of 'modernism', is itself full
of cadavers. The 'death of the author', of 'grand narratives', of
'art', and what have you. Post-postmodernism, or post-everything, if such a sad state would ever be allowed to exist, would
be the land of the zombies; a living death.

Modernism was all about progress but not necessarily *development,* as we will discuss in some detail in the very last chapter.
Modernist utopia was predominantly economical and technological, but also social and political. The utopia lasted roughly
from the second half of the eighteenth century to the second half
of the twentieth. By the beginning of the last century, artists and
literati were already littering the cabarets and salons of Zurich,
Berlin and Paris, where anti-art manifestos were read and Dada
performances were put on.

Dada was the first anti-art movement and perhaps the first
politically charged counter-culture. Surely, the Bohemians and
the Dandies and other offshoots of nineteenth century
Romanticism were already thriving at the fringes of the

mainstream culture of their times, but Dadaists were the true proto-postmoderns that inhabited the space created by the spiritual emptiness of the first great war, and declared: "Da Da Da."

By the end of the second Great War the utopias of progress were given a kiss of life by the Cold War. The promise of economic, technological and social progress sustained and continued to capture the popular imagination thanks largely to the contradiction that emerged between the capitalist thesis and its socialist anti-thesis. The Hegelian engine of progress was in the driver's seat of History once again.

The arms race of the Cold War is rightly credited for many of the technological innovations that populated the West post-Second World War, and thus for the hope for a better future in the popular imagination.

ca. AD 610: End of Prophethood

O Ali, to me you are what Aaron was to Moses except that there will be no prophet after me[12]

It was Fukuyama not Mohammed that declared the end of the history as we know it, and hence the promise of eternal bliss ever after for the West. But before Fukuyama there were a string of Abrahamic religions that signaled the beginnings of ends with Moses, Jesus and Mohammed.

All three great monotheistic religions shared the common eschatological worldview that life began with the *word* that created the world and will end with its destruction and resurrection of the dead, followed by the final judgment and eternal afterlife. The uniqueness of the Mohammedian message among the three monotheistic religions is its explicit proclamation of its finality. The Quadratic declaration that Mohammed is the 'seal of the prophets' is commonly interpreted as the confirmation of the truth of the previous prophets, but also that he is the last of the God's messengers, and there will be no new messenger after him.

The *linear* eschatology with a clearly marked beginning and end, which is common to all three great monotheistic religions, is to be reinterpreted and repeated in Western thought throughout history. Fukuyama's premature declaration of the victory of the liberal-capitalist system over all other socio-economic organizations of life on earth was only the last in the line of philosophical speculation that characterized the Western way of thinking about life and time.

This linear history of time is to be found in different forms in different contexts in modern thought, and can be contrasted with *cyclical* eschatology of non-Western traditions, which emphasizes the eternal recurrence, where an end of an age is always followed by the beginning of a new one. We will return to this point in the final chapter to suggest that this way of looking at life has a better potential in helping us in understanding the social and the future economic organization of life on earth.

Before turning to the great nineteenth century philosopher Hegel, in whose thought the idea of progress is crystallized for the first time in human history, we will first have a brief look at another age that came to an end, the Age of Discovery.

Age of Discovery

There is probably no other time of such a crucial significance to the forms of socio-economic – as well as biological – life on earth than the great explorations and discoveries that took place between the fifteenth and seventeenth centuries. In this relatively (compared to the history of the evolution of the human species) short period, the landmass of Eurasia that comprised the known world was linked and integrated with the rest of the earth, the Americas, Africa, Oceania, resulting in the globalization of the world for the first time in its history. Certainly, it wasn't for the first time that these parts of the earth were explored and 'discovered'.

It is now generally agreed that the gap between Eurasia and Americas was bridged for the first time by the inhabitants of Siberia. The Bering land bridge that joined the two shores of the Bering Strait between Alaska and Siberia during the Pleistocene ice age was crossed at least 10,000 years ago before the landing of the first Europeans on the shores of the Americas, while it was still frozen. There may have been other landings on the shores of the Americas by seagoing coastal settlers earlier than that.

> The *Pleistocene Ice Age* spanned the period from 2.5 million to 12,000 years before the present day.

However, none of the previous migrations are comparable in impact to the series of dramatic events that took place after the arrival of Christopher Columbus to the Americas in 1492. Columbus' landing has resulted in, for better or worse, hitherto unseen levels of exchange of animals, plants, culture, communicable diseases, ideas and peoples between the Old and the New Worlds, known as the 'Columbian Exchange', changing the natural and social ecology of our world for good (or bad).

Among the myriad of other legacies of the Age of Discovery is the decimation of the most of the peoples of the South and North Americas and their ways of life by diseases brought to the colonized lands from the old world, enslavement, and looting. Africa, and Australia, and later parts of Asia too had to bear the consequences of the loot of their human and natural resources by their conquistadors.

Not all of the consequences of the age of the exploration and discovery had been negative, certainly not for Europe. The emergence of merchant capitalism in Spain and Portugal, the first of the European powers involved in the exploration and

exploitation of the new lands discovered, was a direct consequence of the pillage of the riches of the colonized peoples,
especially the gold and silver found in the South America.
Holland, England, France and other major European powers
would soon follow suit. As we will see, from a Hegelian
perspective such a development could be seen as necessary.

End of the Age of Discovery: Deskilling and Plasticization

Primitive forms of accumulation of capital by trade and looting
preceded the industrial mode of production. The merchant
capitalism of the fifteenth and sixteenth centuries of Europe, as
the name implies, was not based on the manufacturing industries, but on the import of raw materials and precious metals
from colonies to metropolises, where they were lightly processed
and exported to other parts of the world.

The merchants not only acted as intermediaries between the
metropolis and its colonies. Wealthy merchant-adventurers
founded the early forms of banking houses that in time helped
integrate more and more of industrialized processing into the
economy. This development slowly transformed merchant
capitalism into industrial capitalism in the eighteenth century,
which accelerated the accumulation and concentration of capital.
The 'free-market' industrial capitalism in turn gave way to
'monopoly' or more correctly 'oligopoly' capitalism with the
concentration of wealth in the late nineteenth century in the
hands of a small number of banking houses and industrial
cartels. This trend continues today with increasing areas of
economic life being dominated by large corporations.

One of the most important consequences of the Age of
Discovery for our purposes is the de-skilling of the native
cultures. I am not referring here to the physical decimation of the
natives but to the loss of the ways of life by the changes imposed
on them. The change of ways of life is not simply the substitution

of one culture for another. Skilled communities have slowly been replaced by de-skilled collections of individuals as pre-manufactured goods took the place of handcrafted ones. To put it simply, pre-fabricated plastics have come to replace the artifacts skillfully carved out of nature.

The main legacy of this age of explorations was the invention of capitalism, or more precisely, transition from the feudal economy to capitalist forms of economic relations. With a twist of fate, the mechanism responsible for the de-skilling of native cultures will return, like a boomerang, back to the colonizing peoples to hunt them. As we will return to in Chapter 5, one of the most important characteristics of the capitalist mode of production is mechanization and de-skilling of the labor force.

Circumnavigating the Globe

Another significant event of the Age of Discovery is the circumnavigation of the globe for the first time by Magellan. In the summer of 1518, Magellan with his fleet of five ships sailed from Seville, Spain and in October 1520 reached the tip of the South American mainland where he found a canal that connects the Atlantic Ocean to the Pacific Ocean. The canal was later named after him as the 'Strait of Magellan'. His was the first expedition to sail from the Atlantic Ocean into the Pacific. The expedition continued across the Pacific, returning back to Spain in 1522. Magellan, however, was killed before the completion of the expedition in a battle in the Philippines with a local chieftain in April 1521.

The earth has been since circumnavigated countless times by sea. The first aerial circumnavigation of the world was undertaken in 1924 by a fleet of four planes of the United States Army Air Service. Only two of the four airplanes managed to complete the 44,000 km journey in 175 days

The first nonstop unrefueled circumnavigation of the earth by plane was achieved by Dick Rutan, an American aviator, who in

1986 co-piloted with Jeana Yeager an aircraft built by Burt Rutan, brother of Dick, named 'Voyager'.

On July 3, 2002, Steve Fossett became the first person to solo circumnavigate the earth in a balloon. He travelled from Northam, Western Australia, and returned to Queensland, Australia in 14 days covering a distance of 33,000 km, beating Sir Richard Branson, founder of the Virgin group, on the way. Both Fossett and Rutan collaborated with Branson in a number of world record attempts, which will be discussed in Chapter 3 when we analyze the innovation strategy of Branson and the Virgin brand.

Afro-Asiatic Age of Discovery

The first signs of substantial knowledge and capital accumulation emerged, however, earlier, around the ninth century, in the medieval Islamic world. The level of development in arts and sciences was so high that one would expect capitalism and industrialization to emerge in the Middle East several centuries before the Age of Discovery and the industrialization that followed suit in the West.

Such polymaths as Al-Khwarizmi (780-850), Al-Kindi (801-873), Al-Farabi (872-950), Ibn Sina, or as known in the West, Avicenna (981-1037), and many others made a great many contributions to the knowledge stock of mathematics, geography, medicine, astronomy, and other sciences. This period of progress in human history is comparable to that of the Renaissance in late fourteenth century Europe. The Renaissance was in fact a direct heir of the 'Islamic Golden Age' according to many.

The expansion of knowledge in the sciences was accompanied and indeed preceded by the explorations of much of the Old World in the period between the seventh to fourteenth centuries, known sometimes as the 'Muslim Age of Discovery' or 'Afro-Asiatic Age of Discovery' to underline the contributions made by Central Asian and North African scholars and explorers to the scientific and cultural progress made in this period.

Such travelers as Al-Idrisi (1100-1165), and Ibn Battuta (1304-1368), near-contemporary of Marco Polo (1254-1324) and one of the greatest travelers ever, explored most of the Old World, which helped establish a proto-global economy. However, by the time of Marco Polo, the Golden Age of Islam was waning.

End of the Muslim Age of Discovery

There are numerous factors that contributed to the decline and end of the Islamic Golden Age, including the raids of the Crusaders in the eleventh century from the West, then from the East by the armies of Genghis Khan a couple of centuries later. Ironically, while Genghis Khan's armies rampaged most of the great cities of the Islamic world, *Pax Mongolica* established under his rule made the land expeditions of the Venetian explorer Marco Polo possible, whose adventures in turn inspired Columbus.

What is of particular interest among the factors that contributed to the decline of the Golden Age of Islam for our present discussion is the attitude towards innovation ('bidah') in Islam. Two different kinds of 'innovations' are distinguished by the Muslim clergy: innovation in religious matters, and innovation in worldly matters. The first was unequivocally condemned. The second was generally allowed on the condition that they did not violate the Islamic law or 'Sharia'.

The sphere of influence of religious matters, however, extended to a large part of intellectual life, and after the early groundbreaking work on Ancient Greek philosophy by Avicenna and others, speculative philosophy and free intellectual debate were increasingly suppressed. This must have been a contributing factor to the decline of science and innovation and the eventual end of the Golden Age of Islam.

It would, however, be more accurate, in my view, to explain the decline of the Islamic civilization in terms of the sudden rise of European powers, the so-called 'European Miracle' from the fifteenth century onwards, which owes much of its success to the discovery of the new territories and trade routes during the European Age of Discovery. Unsurprisingly, Avicenna's and other Muslim scholars' work on Ancient Greek philosophy had contributed greatly to the emergence of Europe as a major power in the Late Middle Ages.

The building up of strain in the relationship between free philosophical thought and scholastic dogmatism in the Islamic world came perhaps most forcefully to the surface in the work of al-Ghazali (1058-1111), who argued strongly for the supremacy of scripture over philosophical speculation, which proved to be highly influential among Muslim clerics and the political elite. Ghazali's arguments resonated strongly in the Islamic clergy (ulema) arguably because the concept of finality and self-sufficiency of Islam had been firmly established before him among the ulema.

It is worth noting that Islamic civilization ended not because of de-skilling in the Muslim communities, as was the case for the indigenous communities of the Americas and Africa, but because they were *out skilled*. The doctrine of the finality and self-sufficiency of Islamic knowledge seemed to play a secondary role in the decline, in that, after the *de facto* economic decline due to the discovery of alternative trade routes and the invention of the capitalist mode of economy by the European competitors, the doctrine of self-sufficiency functioned as an obstacle to prevent any attempt at reformation of the society; a trend which continues to constrain development of much of the Islamic world today.

Collapsing New Buildings[13]

It seems that the Islamic civilization was conceived from the beginning as a static system that would resist any significant internal change, much in the same vein of all the other medieval societies of the West and the East. This meant that only a small portion of the society, the artisans, merchants, soldiers, and select number of political and religious elites were in possession of highly developed cognitive and physical (manual) skills. A static medieval society designed to last forever, naturally, had no incentive or means to establish a highly developed skills base.

While the end of the medieval Islamic civilization came, as we have seen, primarily from without, that is, as a result of out skilling by their European competitors, the current decline of the Western civilization, as we will see in more detail in Chapter 5, comes from within, that is, de-skilling by automation that drives the expansion of Capital.

While the causes of decline stemmed in different localities (within and without) in the cases of medieval Islam and the contemporary West, the progress of the disease that caused the decline in both cases manifests a similar pathology: *Vertical Epistemic Development* at the expense of *Horizontal Ontic Development*.

The main means of development of knowledge in Islamic philosophy were 'Kalam' and 'Falsafa'. Kalam was the study of Islamic theological principles through a sort of primitive 'dialectic' that took the form of dialogue. We will return to examine the dialectic mode of inquiry later in this chapter when we look at the influence of Hegel on modern thought. Falsafa was a freer form of thinking about theological problems and more generally the questions about existence, influenced to a large extent by Greek philosophy.

Both forms of thinking came under attack from the orthodox clergy, and as we briefly discussed earlier, were suppressed eventually. It is easy to see how scholastic thought confiscates the development of scientific knowledge, and consequently distorts our understanding of the nature of reality when reduced to hermeneutic study of scripture. However, the problem is more general than that.

One could liken 'theoretical' knowledge to a high-rise building, a skyscraper. The taller it grows does not necessarily mean that it gets better at approximating the reality. On the contrary, the taller it gets, the less ground it covers per meter of its height. Or, conversely, the taller it grows, the more weight it imparts on each square meter of the *real* estate it is built on, which eventually results in its collapse.

There are two main kinds of theories of *truth*: 'correspondence' and 'coherence' theories. According to the correspondence theory, the truth of a given piece of knowledge is established by how well it reflects the reality. Or, if you prefer, by the measure of its coverage of a given ground – much like the extent of a foundation of a building that takes up a certain amount of ground. The coherence theory, on the other hand, states that truth is purely an internal matter. A theory is true if the statements that make it up are consistent with each other, i.e. coherent, regardless of how well it corresponds to the reality.

This is a theme we will return to discuss in the last chapter. Suffice to note here that any system of thought that passes a certain level of complexity ends up distorting the reality by cutting itself off from the ground it is built on – a process that sows the seeds of its eventual downfall. As one grows a theory by adding new statements to it, or builds a higher building by adding more storeys to it, a point will be reached sooner or later where the theory is no longer coherent, or the building, structurally sound. I call this type of growth Vertical Epistemic (theoretical) Development: internal growth of knowledge by addition of new statements *without changing the external world* at the same rate of its growth.

The great twentieth century mathematician Gödel (1906 - 1978) formalized the mechanism of this process. As the complexity of a formal system such as arithmetic increases, it eventually produces its own paradoxes and contradictions that cannot be resolved from within. The emerging problems thus need to be tackled from without. This could be likened to moving a slowly yielding building to a new, firmer site – a topic that we will return to in Chapter 5.

The 'skyscraper' is the true image of knowing, and more generally of existing, in the age of the capitalist mode of production. We will see in Chapters 4 and 5 that this way of living has been showing signs of gradual decline, as observed in Western art and culture, economy, and indeed science, since the beginning of the last century. This is, perhaps, most expressively declared in the title of Oswald Spengler's (1880-1936) famous work *The Decline of the West*, or *The Downfall of the Occident* (depending on the preference for the two possible translations of the original German title) published in 1918.

The moral of all this is that too much vertical theoretical growth will eventually bring downfall. While the work of internal vertical growth of knowledge is often necessary, past a certain point it brings a myopic vision that distorts the view of reality, as well as bringing about internal contradictions and inconsistencies, unless accompanied by an equivalent amount of horizontal development work on the 'real estate' upon which the structures of knowledge are built. However, 'real estate' should be understood here not just as the sum of the land and the infra-structure on it, but as the sum of all material (natural and artificial) and *human* resources. I call this type of growth *Horizontal Ontic Development*, which actually changes the world instead of merely providing a theory of how it works or changes!

Ideally, the two types of development should work in tandem, each informing the other, and taking the lead as necessary. But this is not always the case. I'll argue in Chapter 5 that the present state of the world is a point in case of the one-sided growth of theoretical knowledge at the expense of the practice of changing the world and the practical knowledge that ensues from it.

Lessons from the Ends of the World

The archetype of cyclical process of birth, rise and downfall of empires and civilizations tells a simple story: the end of a civilization that has lost its touch with reality is always followed by a birth of a new one that breaks a new ground elsewhere.

If a single lesson is to be taken home from the discussion thus far it is the following: vertical growth of knowledge, that is, addition of new knowledge consistent with the system, increases the internal complexity of the system, however, in the long run it yields diminishing returns as each added new piece fails to develop at the same rate the material and human base, or the real estate, that sustains it.

While medieval Islamic civilization, towards the end of the fourteenth century, did not have the means to support the development of its real estate, in particular, its pool of skills base, contemporary societies today do: hence the reason for my hope for a better world, globally. This theme is taken up in a greater depth in the last chapter.

The End of History: Here Comes Hegel

Medieval Islam tried to freeze ˋits own development by announcing its finality from the beginning. While it prevented building of ever-taller buildings of theoretical knowledge that introduce internal contradictions, it continued the development of its own metaphysical thought, which was by definition cut off from the material reality. The case of the contemporary West is different; it covers too little ground (*real* estate) for the dizzying heights of its theoretical buildings and skyscrapers.

The end of the Western civilization is announced neither by clergymen, nor Spengler at the beginning of the twentieth century, but by an early nineteenth century philosopher Georg Wilhelm Friedrich Hegel (1779-1831). This announcement of the end, like the doctrine of the self-sufficiency of Islam, was a reassuringly positive one. Hegel held a *teleological* view of history that 'History' has a purpose or ultimate goal: it progresses from primitive state to a more advanced one. For Hegel, the locus of the progress of History shifted from the East to the West and culminated in the Germanic Protestant society of the nineteenth century.

Hegel's philosophy of history is concerned with the development of 'Geist', variously translated to English as 'Mind' or 'Spirit'. Hegel argued that Geist moves towards to self-awareness and realization, fulfilling God's original plan. Hegel's concept of Geist may be read as broadly equivalent to the Christian view of God. Arguably, Hegel understood Geist also in more secular terms as social mind or a trans-individual or collective form of consciousness.

According to Hegel, Spirit develops and transforms itself as it moves through a succession of historical stages: empires and civilizations are formed, develop and achieve a level of perfection. However, there is only relative or temporary perfection. It does not last for very long. Every perfection hides within it the seeds of its self-destruction. As soon as some level of perfection is attained, Spirit destroys itself to be reborn out of its ashes anew. With every turn of the spiral, Geist marches towards its ultimate destination, as it grows stronger and more advanced than its previous incarnations.

Through this process of self-negation and rebirth Spirit drives the spiral of historical progress, which ends in complete self-realization and self-understanding. To characterize this process Hegel used a variety of triadic expressions, such as 'thesis', anti-thesis' and 'synthesis', and 'affirmation', 'negation' and 'negation of negation'. In this dialectical formulation, thesis is negated by anti-thesis; the resulting contradiction is then cancelled out by a new synthesis, which subsumes both.

To illustrate this idea, let us consider a given historical epoch such as medieval feudal kingdoms. Medieval kingdoms can be seen as a thesis that represents a particular ideal of economic and political organization of society. This thesis was contradicted and challenged by the emergence of the anti-thesis of merchant capitalism that we briefly discussed earlier. The feudal kingdoms were negated and destabilized by the new ways of trade and economy brought by merchant capitalism. The contradiction between the old and the new economic orders was eventually resolved by the development of industrial capitalism and the formation of new nation states and which established a new synthesis. This synthesis subsumed the both forms of socio-economic organization that preceded it. Neither feudalism nor merchant capitalism was completely destroyed, however. Their residues were (and still are) found in the politico-economic composition of the nation states of nineteenth century Europe, in which they continued to live a marginal life under the new order. The industrial capitalism of the nineteenth century has been since developed into new forms, such as 'monopoly capitalism' and 'finance capitalism' in the first and second halves of the twentieth century respectively – a transformation driven mainly by its own internal conflicts and contradictions.

For Hegel, nineteenth century Germany represented the ideal society, the ultimate realization of Geist. The subsequent turn of events belies Hegel's belief in the end of History as nineteenth century Prussian Germany. Karl Marx (1818-1883) was one of the first to realize this. His materialist dialectics turned Hegel's idealism upside down by putting the material economic relations in place of Spirit. For him History would end with the subsumption of capitalism in a higher form of socio-economic organization that he called communism.

For others, such as Francis Fukuyama, Hegel's ideas heralded the final victory of liberal capitalism over all other socio-economic forms of organization with the fall of the Soviet Union and her allies at the end of the 1980s. However, this turned out to be a premature declaration too. By the look of conflicts and clashes that History has since witnessed, Hegel's spiral of

forward march seems to be far from arrival at its final destination. The current so-called 'credit crunch', which in fact is a
structural crisis of finance capitalism, should have made that
clear for everyone. We will return to the current state of the world
economy in the context of innovation and the new economy in
the very last chapter of the book.

Dialectics Old and New

One attraction of dialectics is that it is a universal way of thinking
about change in the world. It is the only form of logic to be found
in both the Orient and the Occident. It is also the oldest form of
logic. It preceded Aristotle's (384 BC-322 BC) syllogism, which is
the mother of all modern logics prevalent in scientific thinking.
Heraclitus of Ephesus (535-475 BC) was a pre-Socratic
philosopher who lived in Ephesus in Anatolia. He is famous for
the dialectic maxim 'you cannot step twice into the same river.'
Forms of dialectical thinking were also found in ancient China
and India, and other civilizations.

I find dialectical logic useful as a tool for understanding the
historical development of our planet as well as envisioning its
future. As I will argue in the last chapter it is, however, more
fruitful to think about our past and future in terms of the cyclic
process of death and rebirth instead of linear progression to a
finality where nothing changes afterwards. As Eastern wisdom
suggests in countless fables and parables, death is not the
opposite of life but of rebirth. Every death is a beginning of a new
life, not an end.

Hegel's ideas also turned out to be useful in understanding
the stagnation the art world currently seems to be experiencing,
which I touched upon briefly in the first chapter. We will have a
look at the claims of the 'End of Art' as we know it, and the
emerging new forms of 'artscience', in the context of invention
and innovation in Chapter 4.

3

Innovation Lessons for New Economy Entrepreneurs

• On Forgetting to Know • Carnivalesque • And the King Shook His Bottom • Popular Pleasures • Bawdy Branson and Hypersexed Virgin • Talking to Me? Virgin Hailing Itself • Virgin Territory: Space • A Virgin Strategy • Microsoft: The Fifth Commandment • Microsoft's Preemptive Strategy: Wait and Imitate • Death by Ugly Consumerism • Apple Aesthetics • Being-in-the-World • The New Age of Discovery: The Cyber Frontier • Innovation Lessons: Summary

On Forgetting to Know

What makes a good innovator? Is there a general innovation *strategy* applicable to all? The answer to the latter depends partly on the answer to the former question, which is surprisingly straightforward: it is the same stuff that makes a *bad* economist.

Paul Krugman, a Nobel laureate in economics, asks in *A Country is not a Company*[14] why economists do not make good businesspeople and vice versa. Here is the short answer:

> Because a corporate leader succeeds [unlike the economist] not by developing a general theory of the corporation … There have been some business greats who have attempted to codify what they know, but such attempts have almost always disappointing.

Does innovation need a strategy? Yes, but as long as you understand 'strategy' not as a mere plot, a mental plan, or a mind game, but as 'the art or skill of using *stratagems*' and '*making do* with the means available'. I repeat myself. Is there a general *innovation strategy* applicable to all? There are different strategies for innovation, perhaps, an indefinite number of them. We will see a few in this chapter. However, they all share a common denominator, which will be elucidated in the rest of this chapter. It is likely that all other possible innovation strategies share the same denominator with the exemplars discussed in this chapter.

Why not say upfront what I will say in the end. The general strategy for innovation consists of the following maxim: 'stop knowing and start acting'. In other words it consists of *giving up* theorizing and taking up hands-on practical aesthetic *ontic development work*.

The innovation strategies that we will discover in this chapter range from 'popular pleasures', to use the words of John Fiske, Professor of Communication Arts and a well-known theorist of popular culture,[15] to 'ontic shifts of discovery'. The common denominator shared by all is 'a shift from cognition to activity' in the words of Fred Newman and Lois Holzman, renegade psychotherapists and political activists, and inventors of 'social therapy', an activity-theoretic approach to therapy and learning.[16] To put it simply and squarely, innovation is a game of 'learning by doing', while forgetting the old ways of doing things.

While there are many strategies for innovation, there is practically one sure way to kill it: *non-innovation by pre-emption*. I call this non-strategy *hypercritical*, or perhaps I should say *hypocritical self-abstinence*, which I will ponder on later.

I confess: I have just committed non-abstinence from the popular pleasure of ridiculing the great and the mighty. And I intend not to, in the rest of this chapter, deny to myself, or to you, the worldly pleasures of the profane, the grotesque and the excessive.

Carnivalesque

'Carnivalesque' is a term invented by the Russian critic Mikhail Bakhtin (1895-1975) in his analysis of the work of François

Rabelais (ca. 1493-1553), major Renaissance writer of fantasy, satire, grotesque, and bawdy jokes and songs. The Wikipedia entry on carnivalesque has the following on it:

Bakhtin traces the origins of the carnivalesque to the concept of carnival, itself related to the Feast of Fools, a medieval festival originally of the sub-deacons of the cathedral, held about the time of the Feast of the Circumcision (1 January), in which the humble cathedral officials burlesqued the sacred ceremonies, releasing 'the natural lout beneath the cassock.'

In his *Problems of Dostoevsky's Poetics* (1929) and *Rabelais and His World* (1965), Bakhtin likens the carnivalesque in literature to the type of activity that often takes place in the carnivals of popular culture. In the carnival ... social hierarchies of everyday life—their solemnities and pieties and etiquettes, as well as all ready-made truths—are profaned and overturned by normally suppressed voices and energies. Thus, fools become wise, kings become beggars; opposites are mingled (fact and fantasy, heaven and hell).

Toreador Song is one of the most popular arias from Georges Bizet's famous *opéra comique*, Carmen. Sung by the matador Escamillo, it describes various situations in the ring, the cheering of the crowds and the fame that comes with victory.

Carmen premiered at the Opéra-Comique of Paris on 3 March 1875, but its opening run was denounced by the majority of critics. Bizet died of a heart attack, aged 36, on 3 June 1875, never knowing how popular *Carmen* would become.

(From Wikipedia:
http://en.wikipedia.org/wiki/Carmen)

Your toast, I render it unto you
Sirs, sirs, for along with the soldiers
Yes, the Toreadors can understand;
For pleasures, for pleasure they fight!
"Pour plaisirs, pour plaisirs ils ont les combats!"
The arena is full, it is the feast day
The arena is full from top to bottom.
The spectators, losing their heads,
The spectators begin a big fracas!
Apostrophes, cries, and the uproar
Grows into a furor!
Because it is a celebration of courage!
It is the celebration of people with heart!
Go! On guard! Go! Go! Ah!
(From Wikipedia:
http://en.wikipedia.org/wiki/Toreador_Song)

And the King Shook his Bottom

Richard Branson is prototypical of popular strategists employing a variety of tactics that include challenging authority, orchestrating carnivalesque spectacles, 'taking on the big ones' and round-the-world adrenaline pumped adventures, pulling off all sorts of publicity tricks, or occasionally, pulling down his pants.

But without a coherent framework, a strategy, all these publicity stunts could have exploded in his hands. This is what happens when one does not have a clear *vista*. This is what happened when Bill Gates appeared in an ad campaign for the ill-fated Windows Vista in 2008.

The commercial featured Bill Gates and TV sitcom star Jerry Seinfeld. The most memorable scene of the commercial was saved until the end where Gates – in response to an inquisitive Seinfeld's words of wisdom: '...are they [meaning Microsoft] ever going to come out with something that will make our computers moist and chewy like cake so we can just eat them while working?' – faint-heartedly wiggles his bottom. Ah, toreador ahh... it was meant to be 'celebration of people with heart! Go! On guard! Go! Go! Ah!'

The Vista was to be abandoned for numerous reasons in 2009, just over two years after its general release, and merely a year after the ill-fated multimillion dollar advertising campaign that featured Gates and Seinfeld. It shouldn't have been too hard to second-guess this eventuality given the public reception of the campaign. Here are some random quotes from blogs:

> I can't figure out where Microsoft's going with its new ad with Bill Gates and Jerry Seinfeld, which Ben Romano on his blog. It's one of those desperately seeking-quirky ads that begs for interpretation. There's Jerry offering Bill a bite of his churro, then talking about the size of Bill's shoes. There's a knowing look, and a brief shower scene. A little bit later they're both walking around holding churros. Yikes – Brier Dudley[17]
>
> To be completely honest... I thought the ad was selling shoes? – *mickice*
>
> I have seen the commercial and it's just plain dumb. It makes no kind of sense, It clearly demonstrates how clueless and out of touch these guys are with the mass public. – *Solid_Squirrel*[18]

No doubt, Branson has always been a better shaker. The launch of Virgin Atlantic in 1984 amid media stunts and libido-powered slogans shook the precarious equilibrium established between the aviation dinosaurs on the two sides of the Atlantic, British Airways, TWA, and Pan Am. The latter two have since gone extinct; a finality, which was probably not totally unrelated to the success of Virgin Atlantic.

The problem with Microsoft seems to be that it has gotten into the habit of second-guessing after the fact, be it window-based user interfaces, game consoles, search engines, or publicity stunts. We will return to the case of Microsoft later. Let us continue in the meantime with innovation strategies based on *popular pleasures* and *carnivalesque spectacles*.

Popular Pleasures

Fiske speaks of 'evasive strategies' and 'productive pleasures' in discussing the role of pleasure in culture, in particular, 'popular culture'. 'Populace' should not be confused with 'mass', or 'popular culture' with 'mass culture'.

Popular was originally a legal and political term, from Latin *popularis* that means 'belonging to the people'. Popular culture is created by the people, for the people, bottom-up, whereas, mass culture is manufactured top-down by the people for profit. It is based on a culture of *making* meanings instead of accepting ready-made ones, as Fiske puts it. It is a culture centered on the *body* as a site of both evading disciplinary forces of control, exercised from without and top-down, and producing one's own meanings by, what Fiske calls, 'excorporation' – the process of *making do* by appropriating and transforming the symbolic meanings associated with commodities and any other resource available. Popular culture, in short, is the *folk* culture of industrial societies.

Popular culture, contrary to popular belief due to confusion with mass culture, is a domain of both resistance and evasion, and creation and invention. Popular pleasures are and have always been a fertile ground for culture clash and invention out of necessity.

The following characteristics of *popular pleasures* need to be born in mind:

- Popular pleasures exist only in its practices and contexts, in the sense that they are not based on abstract ideas or factual knowledge.

- They are centered on the *body* and socially constructed meanings.
- Popular pleasures are not *merely* consumed.
- The participants in popular activities are directly involved in the production of pleasure.
- There are two main sources of popular pleasures.
- Those that are based on evading and challenging the *disciplinary* top-down social forces, and those based on appropriating and transforming *hegemonic* meanings.
- The pleasure in evading disciplinary forces manifests itself with the release of suppressed psychic and natural instincts, 'the natural lout beneath the cassock' so to speak – as in the practice of head banging of rock fans, or rowdiness of football fans, or, for that matter, in the practice of wiggling the bottom or pulling one's pants off as in the case of business moguls!
- Popular pleasures include the search for an adrenalin rush, such as in the case of *extreme sports* of rock climbing or bungee jumping, or round the world expeditions.
- Popular pleasures are often found at the moment of breakdown of culture into nature as in sudden surges of amorous emotions and sexual desires, or in loosing one's head in frenzy of religious or spiritual ecstasy.
- Popular pleasures are often accompanied with passionate interests and fierce attractions for strange and beautiful things, for the *sublime* inexplicable *quality* hidden in things.
- Popular pleasures are also found in hopeless bids and challenges put forward in attempts to conquer death and nothingness, and the yearning for immortality.
- There is pleasure in creating one's own meaning, and resisting socially dominant meanings.
- Symbolic resistance and creativity manifests itself in

popular culture often through *excorporation,* that is, appropriation and transformation of commodities and things in a bid to create one's own meanings out of them – for there is pleasure in creating one's own culture, a *personal* virtual reality, a cultural 'vat' full of nutritious and relevant experiences, so to speak.

- The process of excorporation is practical and hands-on.

An example of *ex*corporation is the tearing of new jeans by teenagers, and adult rock fans alike as an expression of angst and rebellion; a typical act of modification of the codified meanings of a pair jeans in a bid to express a personal meaning... well, at least, that was the case in the 60s and 70s before the 'torn jean' is *in*corporated back to the fashion industry. Is it possible to re-tear pre-torn jeans?

- Popular forms of expression of personal meanings often take the form of *bricolage* (construction or creation of a 'work' from a diverse range of things which happen to be available).
- Popular pleasures are opposed to elite pleasures.
- Elite pleasures are derived from passive, *passionless,* disinterested reflection on beauty.
- Highbrow culture is opposite of popular culture; it harbors distant coolness from the aesthetic object.
- It associates culture with knowledge.
- High culture lays claim to universal validity.
- Popular pleasures are bodily and contextual, based on personal experiences that are relevant to particular individuals in particular contexts.

The differences between high and popular cultures are summarized below.

Popular Pleasures versus Elite Aesthetics

POPULAR: Popular pleasures exist only in its practices and contexts, and center on the *body*. Bliss (*jouissance*) occurs at the moment of breakdown of culture into nature:

- Carnivalesque rowdiness (e.g. football, rock fans)
- Evasiveness and challenging authority
- Adrenaline rush
- Youth and working class

ELITE: Elite pleasures derive from cool, distant reflexive contemplation. Bourgeoisie associates culture (high art) with knowledge; pleasure derives from measured reflection:

- Lacking the lived; bodily senses are sites of impure taste
- Valuing expert opinion and taste
- Reflexive contemplation
- Middle and high classes

Bawdy Branson and Hypersexed Virgin

Branson and the libidinal economy of the Virgin brand are the testimony for evasive and productive strategies at play in the business of innovation. Branson is a master of ceremonies and spectacles, of bodily pleasures and adrenalin-powered excesses of the body, as well as the art of appropriating and transforming popular meanings.

His well-orchestrated spectacles could give the wrong impression, of being mere tactics to put himself and his company into the public eye. While Branson's liberal use of libidinal stunts and endorphin-soaked adventures, such as crossing the Atlantic in a powerboat or circumnavigating the world in a hot-air balloon, did generate ample free publicity, there was a deeper method to his apparent appetite for living dangerously, which probably was not obvious to him in Virgin's formative years.

In a speech he gave at the London Leaders' Conference, on 29 November 2006, Branson made clear that he is no theory-man: 'I've never followed business models or what the marketing gurus say. We've developed a fairly thick skin against the criticism of experts.' Note especially the last sentence for our discussion of Microsoft in the latter part of this chapter.

He continued, 'I always agonise about whether the critics are right. It spurs us on to succeed. We call the Virgin approach *Branded Venture Capitalism*. Now the Virgin approach to business is studied at Harvard and INSEAD'. This was a particularly interesting revelation as Branson has always in the past insisted that he had no strategy or business plan. Things seem to have moved on for Branson and company quite a bit since the days of no strategy, no theory.

Branded Venture Capitalism has recently given way for even grander schemes. Lets hear it from Branson: 'Gaia Capitalism is the new Virgin approach to business. We are actively looking for fuels and technology to secure our future. Even with the space venture we are looking to develop space launch systems that use renewable energy sources.'[19]

Talking to Me? Virgin Hailing Itself

Let's start with the 'Branded Venture Capital' approach. The psychology of the masses and how brands tap into the conscious and unconscious desires and wants of consumers are well known. I am not going to go into a detailed analysis of brand psychology. What is interesting in the case of Virgin's approach is not so much its success in tapping and manipulating known and unknown desires and wants, nor its building imaginary relationships between consumers and brands. This is, after all, all successful branding and advertising do.

Pepsi created the concept of the *Pepsi Generation* in the 80s. When an advert declares you as The Pepsi Generation, it speaks to you directly, it hails you, or 'interpellates', in the words of philosopher Louis Althusser (1918-1990).

The speaking voice, in this example 'Pepsi', urges you to identify yourself with a group with certain shared character-istics. In the Pepsi ad this is the youth and those who want to be youthful. By responding positively to the ad at an emotional level, you recognize yourself to belong to a particular identity group, that of the youth and the youthful. The ad succeeds if it makes you think 'that is me'.

What is noteworthy of Virgin is the swapping of the posts of the addresser and addressee in the communication circuit, or rather their *conjoining*. Virgin speaks in a different voice. By a sudden overturn of the order of communication, the interpel-lated (or the addressee), and the interpeller (or the addresser), are mingled and conjoined in Virgin slogans, such as: 'No way BA/AA'.

Here, in challenging the authority of the major UK and US airlines, Virgin suddenly looks innocent again. It is not one of them – the big and the powerful – any more. As if touched by the hand of God, it switches its allegiances and becomes one of us, member of the general public, a born-again virgin!

But, in a sense, it is *indeed* one of us; one of the underdogs, so to speak, a subordinated teenage brat, or more to the point, a rebellious punk rocker, challenging the authority of his parents and other social bores. It cannot be a mere accident that when Branson started Virgin as a record company, one of the first acts he signed up was The Sex Pistols, a prototypical punk rock band dropped by EMI, a record industry dinosaur.

Other examples of Virgin Atlantic hailing itself include such slogans as: 'Virgin, seeks travel companion(s)', 'Mine's Bigger

Than Yours' (on the back of its Airbus A340-600s, because they were the longest passenger aircraft in the world at the time: directed to competitors, such as BA), 'Fly a younger fleet' (an equivocal voice; talking to you, or itself, or both perhaps), 'You never forget your first time' (double-tongued again).

The choice of Virgin Atlantic out of all other Virgin enterprises in this section is not arbitrary. It is one of the most noteworthy success stories of Branson, which also proved to be a stepping stone for his major new enterprises, such as Virgin Galactic and Virgin Fuels, which we will discuss next.

A Virgin Territory: Space

This much wouldn't make Branson such a good innovator, if it weren't for his knack for re-inventing himself as a globetrotter, in the image of the great explorers and adventurers of a bygone age, the Age of Discovery. It may be true that some of his record-breaking, globetrotting 'adventures' are carefully orchestrated publicity spectacles. However, my contention is that publicity stunts, and mere searches for adrenaline rush, would not have got him this far; certainly, not as far as outer space. His knack for cashing in on adrenalin-soaked adventures makes better sense when considered in a wider view of his *popular cultural* strategy for doing business and innovation.

The theme of the vagabond anti-hero on the road is a well-known trope in popular literature. The 'picaresque novel', let's read it from Wikipedia,

is a popular sub-genre of prose fiction, which is usually satirical and depicts, in realistic and often humorous detail, the adventures of a roguish hero of low social class who lives by his or her wits in a corrupt society. As indicated by its name, this style of novel originated in Spain, where it was possibly influenced by Arabic literature...

The best-known example of the picaresque novel, undoubtedly, is *Don Quixote*, written between 1605 and 1615 in the Spanish Golden Age that followed the Reconquista or Re-conquest – the defeat and expulsion of the Moors from the Iberian Peninsula – and the sea voyages of Christopher Columbus to the Americas. When considered that it was written about a century after Columbus' expeditions, it could be read as an elegy for the lost heroic age of discoveries.

Don Quixote and the picaresque novel have a lasting influence on popular culture, ranging from Hollywood road movies to Sergio Leone's 'spaghetti westerns'. It is true that Branson appeals (consciously or not) to such antagonists from popular fiction as Robin Hood and Don Quixote. Indeed, he is a peculiar heady mix of the two. Branson's Don Hood or Robin Quixote persona applies equally well to his bid to transform UK's National Lottery to a 'People's Lottery' as to his more recent 'space travel for the masses'.

Undoubtedly, his ability to take in punches and bounce back in the face of failure (he lost the bid for the lottery, to name but one) has added to his popular charm. Regardless of his sometimes quixotic-sounding quests for conquest of new territories to build his empire, he is certainly no purposeless vagabond.

I will, in fact, argue that Branson's unstoppable reach for outer space has grown bottom-up from his appetite for adrenalin sports and world-record attempts at circumnavigating the globe. His is an admirable demonstration that the popular cultural practice of bottom-up learning and innovation by doing works; works very well indeed. The figure further down in this chapter illustrates how his 'ontic-adventures' have driven the theoretical (epistemic) development of Virgin, from its early no-theory days to its future in 'Gaia Capitalism'. But before looking at that figure in-depth, let us continue with Branson's adventures.

A Virgin Strategy

Branson, when asked in an interview 'How do you keep reinventing yourself?' reportedly said, 'I like to throw myself wholeheartedly into life.'[20] This sentence summarizes handsomely his strategy for business innovation. His is not about ideas. His is about life, with its bodily intensities and passionate interests. If 'life is a stage' as Shakespeare suggested, Branson is a 'stage diving rock fan' who throws himself onto the crowd – or life, made of flesh and bodily fluids – below.

Apparently, life throws back to him ideas and opportunities. This symbiosis makes Branson a true popular strategist in both of the senses connoted by the phrase; a popular figure with the public, and a businessman who *purposefully* searches for derring-do, and carnal encounters with life, as well as, well apparently, close encounters with aliens (!).

Let's trace then his tracks that have led to outer space and Gaia Capitalism. Richard Branson made several world record-breaking attempts:

- In 1985, he failed his attempt at the fastest Atlantic Ocean crossing in a powerboat named 'Virgin Atlantic Challenger'. The boat capsized and was rescued by RAF helicopter, which attracted a lot of media attention.
- In 1986, he succeeded in the same challenge; 'Virgin Atlantic Challenger II' beat the world record by two hours.
- In 1987, he succeeded in becoming the first person to cross the Atlantic in a hot-air balloon, named 'Virgin Atlantic Flyer'.
- In 1991, Branson crossed the Pacific from Japan to Arctic Canada, in a balloon named 'Virgin Pacific Flyer', breaking all existing records. His record was broken in 1995 by Steve Fossett, an American businessman, aviator, sailor, and adventurer.
- In March 2004, Branson set a record for the fastest crossing

of the English Channel in an amphibious vehicle by travelling from Dover to Calais in a Gibbs Aquada.

- In 2008, Richard Branson was forced to abandon his bid to break the transatlantic sailing record in a boat named after his financial services company 'Virgin Money' (good thinking Sir Richard, that it was an unsinkable boat!).
- Between 1995 and 1998 Branson teamed up with Per Lindstrand, a Swedish aeronautical engineer, pilot and adventurer, and Steve Fossett, in his attempt to circumnavigate the globe by balloon. In 1998 they made a record-breaking flight from Morocco to Hawaii, however, they were beaten by Bertrand Piccard, a Swiss psychiatrist and balloonist, and Brian Jones, an English balloonist, who flew around the world non-stop in 'Breitling Orbiter 3' in 1999. In 2002 Steve Fossett became the first person to fly around the world alone, nonstop, in a balloon.
- Branson teamed up with Steve Fossett and Burt Rutan, a distinguished American aviator and industrialist, to build 'Virgin Atlantic GlobalFlyer' that in 2005 broke the world record for the fastest nonstop, unrefueled circumnavigation of the earth in a record time of 67 hours 1 minute. The aircraft was owned and piloted by Fossett, financed by Virgin Atlantic, and built by Rutan's company, Scaled Composites. The previous record was hold by Dick Rutan, brother of Burt, who co-piloted the 'Voyager' aircraft with Jeana Yeager, an American aviatrix, in 1986. Between February 8 and 11, 2006 Fossett flew the GlobalFlyer for the longest aircraft flight in history (41,467 km). Sadly, Fossett died in an air crash on 3 September 2007, flying alone in a small single-engine plane.
- On 21 June 2004 "SpaceShipOne", developed by *Mojave Aerospace Ventures,* a company owned by Microsoft co-founder Paul Allen and Rutan's Scaled Composites, successfully completed the first privately funded human

spaceflight to 100km above the earth, the officially desig-
nated *edge of space*. It won, on 4 October 2004, the $10
million Ansari X PRIZE, promised for the first reusable
manned craft to reach 100 kilometers in altitude twice in a
two-week period with the equivalent of three people on
board and with no more than ten percent of the non-fuel
weight of the spacecraft replaced between flights.
Development costs of the spacecraft, estimated to be $25
million, were funded completely by Paul Allen.

- Branson signed a $21.5 million deal with Burt Rutan in
  2005 for the rights of the SpaceShipOne technology, and the
  'Spaceship Company' was born.
- Later that year, Virgin Galactic announced the beginning of
  'space tourism', by pledging $100 million to build up to
  five spaceships at Rutan's factory in Mohave, California.
  SpaceShipTwo, the first of Virgin Galactic's fleet of spacecrafts, was officially unveiled on 7 December 2009 at
  Mojave Spaceport in California. The Virgin spacecrafts are
  launched at around 50,000 ft. from a jet-powered carrier
  aircraft, known as Vigin MotherShip. The second of the
  planned motherships is named as 'VMS Spirit of Steve
  Fossett'. The first one is named after Branson's mother,
  'VMS Eve'.
- The Virgin Galactic plans to start its passenger-carrying
  private spaceflights in 2011.
- In September 2006, Branson has pledged to invest $3 billion
  in the next 10 years in profits from his travel firms, such as
  Virgin Atlantic and Virgin Trains, toward research into
  renewable energy technologies, signaling the birth of his
  concept of 'Gaia Capitalism'.
- The 'Virgin Green Fund' he established is said to focus 'on
  middle market growth and expansion investment opportunities in the renewable energy and resource efficiency
  sectors including water.' One rumored project is the effort

to develop an alternative 'clean' fuel that would replace existing jet fuels, dubbed as unsurprisingly 'Virgin Fuel'.

- In February 2007, Branson committed, in the spirit of the X-prizes, $25 million to the first person to come up with a way of removing greenhouse gases from the atmosphere.

From crossing the Atlantic Ocean in a power boat to circumnavigating the earth by balloon and airplane, and the flights to the edge of the earth's atmosphere, the track left by Branson's travels tells a remarkable story of *learning by doing* when plotted on a timeline and viewed in hindsight (see the figure below).

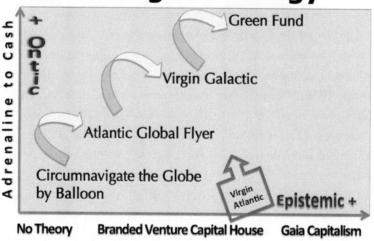

The chart above simply illustrates that ontological shifts to higher realms have paid Branson handsomely, both in new ideas, and in profits. Let me re-iterate from the previous chapters: I use the adjective *ontic* simply to mean 'relating to nature or reality'. 'Ontic shift' in this sense simply means 'a move to a new reality by the discovery of a new set of entities/beings and the relationships between them'. *Ontic* in this sense always presupposes and entails practical activity over theoretical pondering. It requires focusing on the present over reflecting on the past or the future. Worth remembering that popular pleasures and activities are also always practice-oriented and take place in the present.

More concretely then, what the chart illustrates is the correlation between Branson's discovery of new things (people and technology) by practical activity, and the returns yielded by his adventures in ideas and monies.

In the days of record attempts by boat and balloon, in the late 80s and early 90s, it is highly unlikely that Branson had a clear vision of the future of his airline business. However, the string of adventures he had undertaken appears to have put him on the collision course with the right people and right kind of technological inventions, which in time crystallized in the concepts of space tourism, Gaia Capitalism, and the Virgin Green Fund.

The 2006 statement by Branson quoted earlier, 'We are actively looking for fuels and technology to secure our future', leaves little, if any, doubt that by the time of the development of the Virgin Atlantic GlobalFlyer in the early 2000s, he was acutely aware of the need for new technologies to secure the future of his businesses. However, way back in the 90s, at the time of his ballooning adventures, he most certainly had not yet cultivated such a vision.

However, the point is precisely that this apparently-unrelated string of adventures that he has undertaken comprises in fact a consistent logical chain, which has led him from the early days searching for excitement and publicity to his current attitude towards new ways of thinking about his businesses and capitalism in general.

Let me put it more openly: although the relevance of the world record attempts with 'Virgin Atlantic GlobalFlyer' to his new business ventures of 'Virgin Galactic' and 'Virgin Green Fund' is obvious, the relevance of the earlier Branson boating and ballooning adventures is not. My contention, however, is that they are part of the same holistic mindset; without the one the others would not have happened.

Clearly, Branson's reckless search for pleasure and spectacle has guided the development of his thinking, rather than the opposite. Instead of following a mental plot, or a theory, Branson seems to have mastered the art of *serendipity*, that is, stumbling upon fortunate discoveries, while looking for something apparently unrelated. It is perhaps fitting to call his an *oblique*, indeed *evasive*, approach to innovation that is based on discovery of relevant people (Rutan, Fossett) and technologies (SpaceShipOne). Let us read from Virgin Galactic official website:

Our excitement in 2002 on discovering Burt Rutan's plans for SpaceShipOne focused on a number of design features which we believed in their own right could make the vehicles many thousands of times safer than any manned space craft of the past.

Some of the technological innovations that SpaceShipOne embodies include:

- First all-carbon air/spacecraft
- Launched horizontally in the air at 50,000 ft., rather than vertically from the ground like all the other spacecrafts
- Powered by a hybrid rocket motor (crossing more common liquid engines with solid motors)
- Feathered re-entry into the dense atmosphere from the vacuum of space. To prevent overheating of the skin temperature during re-entry the wings of the spacecraft is rotated upwards about 65 degrees. Following re-entry, the feather lowers to its original configuration to enable the spaceship to glide back to the spaceport runway.

The oblique collision courses Branson seems to have purposefully set up appear to have paved the way for one discovery after another that in turn led the development of his theoretical thinking.

The chart given earlier illustrates how his ontological adventures of discovery, of people and technologies, correlate with the development of his business ideas, visions, and innovations. The story of Virgin does not end here, however. Apparently, the next step for Branson and company is to make available the space technology they have developed for out-of-the-atmosphere passenger plane flights, which could in the not too distant future reduce the travel time from New York to Tokyo to an undreamed-of couple of hours.

Virgin Criteria[21]

Virgin would only put its name to a project if it met four out of five criteria:

It must be innovative

Challenge authority

Offer value for money by being better than the competitors

Be good quality

And the market must be growing

Virgin Quotes[22]

In a recent interview Sir Richard was asked: 'did he ever let his heart rule his head?'

He replied: 'All the time – I think that unless you do, you're not going to be a very good business person. The only really good reason for doing things in business is based on what your heart tells you, not your head.'

Popular/bodily/visceral pleasures of Virgin[23]

You've got to challenge the big ones

Keep it casual

Haggle: everything is negotiable

Have fun working

Do the right things for the brand

Smile for the cameras!

Don't lead 'sheep', herd 'cats'

Move like a bullet

Size does matter

Be a common, regular person

Microsoft: The Fifth Commandment

A good example of the opposite of *innovating by doing* is the case of Microsoft. Microsoft is the prototypical epistemologized, hyper self-critical, overly rationalized company when it comes to innovation. Core values of Microsoft are said to include:

1　We act with integrity and honesty.

2　We are passionate about our customers and partners, and about technology.

3　We are open and respectful with others and dedicated to making them better.

4　We are willing to take on big challenges and see them through.

5　We are self-critical, questioning, and committed to personal excellence and self-improvement.

6　We are accountable for commitments, results, and quality to customers, shareholders, partners, and employees. [24]

Allow me to be a little sarcastic: from the look of it, the fifth, 'self-criticism', or as expressed by Kevin Turner, current Chief

Operating Officer (COO) of Microsoft, in a more telling way, a 'healthy degree of insecurity', is the one that really dominates all the others.

Turner, in drawing a comparison between Microsoft founder Bill Gates and his former boss Wal-Mart founder Sam Walton, explained at the company's Small Business Summit in Bellevue that he sees parallels between the two:

> For example, showing a list of Microsoft's corporate traits, he said the software company puts a high value on self-criticism. 'This one is also a Sam Walton trait,' Turner explained. 'He called it having a "divine discontent." Being self-critical without ever getting demotivated is something that's very important.'
>
> Later, talking with reporters, Turner was asked to elaborate on the similarities he sees between them. Among other things, he cited their 'healthy degree' of insecurity about the need to reinvent things, before the competition does. [25]

Let's hear it now from blogs:

> I'm an ex-MS employee (was there 7 years, left in 2009). The biggest issue I can see was that the culture in the company was one of asking tough questions and finding flaws. Something like iPad would have gotten destroyed in a spec review. The culture is less about finding out how to make the product great, but finding all of the way it can fail. And when you enumerate every reason why something can fail, few things (besides the incremental) end up looking good. It's not intentional, but it is a *hypercritical* company. I think it needs to let its hair down... take some risks. – Ken Jackson (italics mine).
>
> yeah... you are right. forgot about that aspect. Spec reviews were 'fun', but also a session of destruction, as you state. it is always too easy to destroy, and thus offer no 'here is

a better idea' – *bb* [26]

Microsoft's Pre-emptive Strategy: Wait and Imitate

Microsoft is hardly associated with groundbreaking innovation. Sure, they have the window-based graphical user interface (GUI); not so imaginatively named as Windows. But that was not the first window-based GUI. Before that there was Apple's Lisa (named after Apple founder Steve Job's daughter), and before that (which, in fact Apple partly copied, or inspired, depending on whose side your sympathies are), there were Xerox PARC's (Xerox's research center at Palo Alto) experimental computers, Alto and Star, which pioneered user interface technologies that have become commonplace in today's personal computers, including the desktop metaphor, window-based graphical user interface, icons, folders, mouse and many other innovations.

Apple unsuccessfully sued Microsoft when Windows 1.0 was released in 1983, on the charges that the 'look and feel' of Lisa, including the use of rectangular, overlapping, and resizable windows, was stolen. A charge to which Bill Gates responded, reportedly:

Well, Steve, I think there's more than one way of looking at it. I think it's more like we both had this rich neighbor named Xerox, and I broke into his house to steal the TV set and found out that you had already stolen it.[27]

Microsoft's reputation as a company that tends to catch-up more than it innovates is not based solely on this episode. Even Microsoft's pre-Windows operating system, MS-DOS, was based on 86-DOS (informally known as the 'Quick-and-Dirty Operating System' or Q-DOS) licensed from a company called Seattle Computer Products. Nintendo and PlayStation then Xbox, Google then Bing – word processor, spreadsheet, web browser – you name it, all of them are invented and developed by someone else first; Microsoft jumped on the bandwagon later and dominated.

It is not that Microsoft is not capable of inventing. In fact it is one the biggest investors in research and development, running a number of excellent research labs around the world, including the UK and China. It is, certain enough, also a big business success churning out profits to the tune of billions every year.

It is not therefore that it cannot invent, but innovate, that is, turn inventions into innovative products. At least, part of the reason for that seems to be that it is good at destroying the aesthetic pleasures and passions associated with new ideas and inventions. In the words of the aforementioned blogger it is too damn good at 'asking tough questions and finding flaws'. It seems that it puts too much faith on the critical faculties, instead of the passions of its employees and their inventions. It seems to prefer the highly profitable business of buying out or imitating others' innovations, and using strong-arm tactics, instead of taking the risk of investing in its own passions, bodily intensities, and aesthetic pleasures. This is why I called this non-innovative strategy *hypercritical* and *hypocritical self-abstinence* earlier.

Could it be a mere coincidence that Kevin Turner, current COO of Microsoft, was the head of Wal-Mart before joining Microsoft, a company which is associated in the minds of many with cheap goods rather than the quality of its products or beauty of its innovations?

Death by Ugly Consumerism

The term 'Black Friday' refers to the day after Thanksgiving Day in the U.S. Traditionally, it is the beginning of the Christmas shopping season. Many retailers open as early as 5am and offer heavy discounts on many types of goods, especially electronics and toys that attract huge crowds. Some of the bigger retailers open as early as midnight on the start of Black Friday and stay open for 24 hours.

More recently, however, it has come to be associated with the tragic events that led to the death of a Wal-Mart temporary employee. On 28 November 2008, chaotic crowds smashed through the Wal-Mart's store in Long Island in search of rock bottom prices. The windows were broken, doors taken off the hinges, and amidst the frantic chaos Jdimytai Damour was trampled to death. An eight-month-pregnant woman and three other shoppers were injured.

Apple Aesthetics

Apple is in many ways the antidote of Microsoft when it comes to innovation. Apple products are regarded by many as being both functional and beautiful. The key to the success of Apple is the stringent design principle it persistently and firmly keeps in place, namely, 'keep it minimal'. This *minimalist* principle permeates everything Apple produces from the more recent iPod and iPhone to its traditional line of computer hardware and software, including the graphical user interface (GUI) that runs on its computers.

True, Apple sometimes pushes the minimalist principle too far, which causes sub-optimal designs and usability problems, such as the lack of the delete key on some of its line of laptops, or the single button mouse, which at one point it tried to make a norm. But, all in all, the aesthetic appeal of Apple always seems to win the hearts of the consumers at the end of the day. The success of Apple innovations seem to rest in large part on the emphasis it lays on the beautiful and the aesthetic. Take the case of the iPhone, one of the many gambles Apple has made, which paid back beautifully.

The iPhone replaces the commonplace interaction patterns of pushing buttons and circling through screen menus found on computer interfaces by touching, tapping, pinching and flicking. The gesture based interaction with the controls of the phone and multitude of applications that run on it increases the aesthetic pleasure one gets out of the interaction, as it is more directly related to natural bodily gestures than pointing and selecting with a mouse.

The increased feeling of 'direct manipulation' deepens the user's experience of *immersion* in the medium, and provides a beautiful embodied interaction, arguably, at the expense of some loss in functionality. This is exactly where Apple has gambled. Obviously, the monolithic screen that replaces the keyboard and buttons crammed in other PDAs and smart phones is not as easy to use when it comes to writing emails more than a few sentences long.

What was said about the iPad by a blogger could easily have been said for iPhone too: 'Something like iPad would have gotten destroyed in a spec review.' However, the aesthetic pleasure that derives from the natural bodily interaction with the device, for most people, seems to more than compensate for its limited usability in writing longer messages. Apple took the risk and reaped the rewards.

But it has not always been happy risk-taking for Apple. There are many Apple products that did not win. They usually won the hearts of the users; they were all beautiful products by design. When they failed, it was usually due to the forbidding price tag to performance ratio. Either it was too expensive for most people, or the performance you got for your money would not justify the expense for those who could afford it. Jobs nevertheless always seemed to go with beauty in the face of such economic inconveniences. The case in point is the Power Mac G4 Cube sold between 2000 and 2001. It was a beautiful and technically advanced machine, inspired by the NeXTcube workstation (see below). It did away with the internal cooling fan, a noisy little part that had always been an annoyance for Jobs. Designed by industrial designer Jonathan Ive, it was one of the few Apple products that was entirely design led. The New York Museum of Modern Art holds a G4 Cube in its collection.

G4 Cube packed a lot of computing power in its small cube-shaped case, but at $2000 for most people it was not powerful enough for that price tag. Although it failed commercially, its successor Mac Mini released in 2005 proved that it was a powerful and beautiful concept that could have succeeded given the right price tag.

It seems that putting the aesthetic design and sensory experience first was always a good part of Jobs' innovation strategy. Long before iMac and iPhone, Apple Lisa, the predecessor of Mac, was the first computer that sported eye-pleasing fonts, beautiful graphics, and rectangles that had soft curved edges. As we saw earlier, it was the first commercial personal computer to have a GUI similar to modern day computers, instead of a text-based command-line interface. Although it produced beautiful documents hitherto unseen, the staggering price tag of $9,995 in 1983 (over $20K in today's money) meant instant commercial failure. However, the ideas tested and lessons learned in developing an advanced multimedia computer contributed a great deal to the success of future Apple computers.

The Mac, combined with Apple's LaserWriter printer, and then groundbreaking software for designing, previewing, and printing page layouts complete with text and graphics, which has come to be known as *desktop publishing*, proved to be highly popular and has become *de facto* standard among graphic designers, artists and musicians.

Not only the software, everything from the case that houses the electronic circuitry to the packaging are carefully designed by Apple. The minimalist but elegant 'Snow White' design language created for Apple by Hartmut Esslinger, a German industrial designer, had become more or less an industry standard in computer case design from mid-80s to mid-90s.

There are many other Apple firsts in the history of computing, and later in the music business. The common thread that weaves the success story of Apple seems to be, however, the importance Apple has put on quality, aesthetics and design, from its very beginnings. In Jobs' words '...our primary goal here is to make the world's best PCs – not to be the biggest or the richest.'[28]

In May 1985, Jobs was forced to leave the company he co-founded, amidst an industry-wide sales slump and power conflicts with then-CEO of Apple John Sculley. Jobs went to venture on a number of other innovative projects, including another computer company, NeXT Computer, later that same year.

Like the Apple Lisa, the NeXT computer was technologically ahead of its time, but cost-prohibitive. Again, like Lisa, it was not commercially successful, but had a significant impact on the computer industry. Both Apple and Microsoft emulated many of the ideas in NeXT with varying success. In 1996 Apple bought NeXT for $429 million, bringing Jobs back to the company he co-founded.

Being-in-the-World

Philosopher Martin Heidegger (1889-1976) argues that our existence is marked by the condition of *being thrown in the world*, that is, being an inseparable part of it. We split the world into subject and object only when things stop working for us. Take, for example, a hammer. We use it without theorizing about it. Only when it breaks or something goes wrong, we see the hammer as an object lying there. As such our existence, our 'Being-in-the-World', is marked by openness to the possibilities offered by the 'ready-to-hand' entities of the world.

Only by interpreting and understanding the world in terms of the possibilities offered by our ordinary everyday existence, and our pre-theoretical relationship with the ready-to-hand (that is ready to use) entities of the world, can we adequately understand the process of invention and innovation. As the examples in this chapter have illustrated, inventions often occur as a consequence of throwing oneself into the possibilities offered by ready-to-hand entities without comporting oneself toward a plan that has been thought out. This is what most people call serendipity.

Innovation is, then, the knack for seeing in fortuitous discoveries and inventions the hidden potential for introducing new ready-to-hand entities that are pleasurable and relevant to our lives, and enrich our everyday existence.

The Microsoft case discussed earlier makes sense in view of Heidegger's philosophy of Being-in-the-World, and the example of the broken hammer: too much theorizing tends to kill innovation. Remember the folk tale of a centipede that had no trouble walking until asked how he managed all those legs. He started thinking about it and instantly became paralyzed.

The New Age of Discovery: The Cyber Frontier

Let us recall the accident that claimed the life of Steve Fossett aviator, adventurer, and friend of Richard Branson. On 3 September 2007, Fossett took off in a single-engine plane. A few hours later, he was reported missing after the plane he was flying over the Nevada desert failed to return. The search for Fossett began about six hours later. Despite days of intensive searching the remnants of the crash were not found.

On 7 September, Branson and others coordinated efforts to launch a virtual search expedition for Fossett by means of the satellite images of the surrounding territory provided by Google Earth. Later, the search was expanded by *crowdsourcing on* the Amazon Mechanical Turk website. More than 300,000 squares of satellite imagery were scrutinized by up to 50,000 people who had joined the search effort on the Mechanical Turk. The search was not successful. The significance of this story for our purposes is, however, the direction it points for discovery and invention in the bourgeoning brave new cyberworld. We will look at this topic further after exploring the close connection between art, science and innovation in the next chapter.

'Amazon's Mechanical Turk, a *crowdsourcing* web service, is named after an 18th-century chess-playing mannequin dressed as a Turkish man. The mannequin's moves were controlled from within by a chess master using gears and pulleys, but opponents didn't know how it worked …
Today's Mechanical Turk is typically used for tasks ranging from transcribing an audio file to writing a restaurant review.'

http://www.wired.com/software/webservices/news/200 7/09/distributed_search

Innovation Lessons: Summary

Let us summarize our findings in this chapter:

- New inventions and ideas happen all the time; they are part and parcel of everyday life.
- Inventions happen to people who have a knack and the will to discern a qualitative difference that makes a difference to someone in some situation/context.
- Necessity is the mother of all inventions, it is often said, and I accede that the popular saying is true. However, necessities are not always pre-given; they emerge from our state of being thrown in the world; our urge to connect with other Beings, and our openness to the possibilities offered by the ready-to-hand entities of the world.
- Often, but not always, inventions spring from practice rather than following a well-thought-out theory. Being locked in a theory could hamper one's ability to discern sensible differences. This point is an important theme that I will take up in the context of *artscience* experiments in the next chapter.
- Joyful, skilled, playful experimentation in the real world

usually provides a more favorable climate for inventions than controlled laboratory experiments.

- Innovation follows when one sees in an invention the potential for introducing new meaningful differences to the world, which are pleasurable and relevant to others' lives and everyday experiences.

Some innovation principles that are suggested by the examples discussed so far include:

- Prioritize the sensory and the aesthetic.
- Challenge, risk, venture.
- Value popular pleasures.
- Avoid over-rationalizing (hypercriticism kills).
- Another one that will be introduced in the final chapter:
- Populate the world with new entities, bodies, and relationships between them.

4

Information Arts: Artscience Entanglement

• **The End of Art** • **Post-Duchamp Syndrome: This Has Been Done Before** • **Conceptual Art** • **Conceptual Art as Popular Text** • **Information Arts** • **Art or Science** • **Art and Science** • **Artscience: Theory Lock-in**

Art in the age of...

handicraft

machines

information

Art in the Age of Handicraft, Machines, Information:

The Birth of Venus, Sandro Botticelli

((Source: The Yorck Project: 10.000 Meisterwerke der Malerei. DVD-ROM, 2002. ISBN 3936122202. Distributed by

DIRECTMEDIA Publishing GmbH.

http://commons.wikimedia.org/wiki/File%3ASandro_Botticelli_046.jpg)

Fountain, Marcel Duchamp, 1917

(Photo: Micha L. Rieser / Wikimedia Commons / CC-BY-SA-3.0,

http://commons.wikimedia.org/wiki/File%3AFontaine-Duchamp.jpg)

Microvenus, Joe Davis, 1990.

The End of Art

Arguably, the art world is in crisis. Ivan Massow, then-chairman of the Institute of Contemporary Arts (ICA), the premier platform for contemporary art in Britain, reportedly remarked in 2002 that 'Most concept art I see now is pretentious, self-indulgent, craftless tat that I wouldn't accept even as a gift.'[29]

In fact, 'the end of art' has been proclaimed by several critics/theorists in recent decades for different reasons. One such critic is philosopher Arthur Danto, who in *After the End of Art* stated that 'To say that history is over is to say that there is no longer a pale of history for works of art to fall outside of. Everything is possible. Anything can be art.'[30]

The apparent lack of rules is arguably at the root of the crisis in contemporary art echoed by the former chairman of the ICA. Evaluation of artworks has become extremely problematic in recent years. One of the reasons for this is the laissez-faire attitude of 'if someone calls it art it is art' prevalent in postmodern culture.

Post-Duchamp Syndrome: This Has Been Done Before

The beginning of the end of art could be traced to the infamous Frenchman Marcel Duchamp (1887-1968) of 'Fountain' fame.

Born in France, Duchamp was associated with Dadaist and Surrealist movements of his time, and is credited with the invention of 'found art'. The term found art or 'readymade', describes art created from everyday, usually industrial, objects that are not produced for the sake of art, but for a certain utilitarian function, as in the case of the urinal that comprised Duchamp's infamous work, Fountain.

His first famous work, however, was not Fountain. In 1912 he created an oil on canvas painting in a mixed Cubist and Futurist style entitled Nude Descending a Staircase, No. 2. Considered by many a Modernist masterpiece, it depicts an abstract movement of a figure composed of nested, conical and cylindrical elements, assembled together in such a way as to suggest rhythm and movement.

In 1915 Duchamp moved to New York, where he was already a celebrity. In 1916 he co-founded the Society of Independent Artists with a number of American artists. The next year, he submitted Fountain to an exhibition organized by the Society of the Independent Artists entitled, signed with his pseudonym 'R. Mutt'. Although the works in the Independent Artists shows were not selected by a jury the show committee rejected it from the show, insisting that it was *not art*. This caused uproar amongst New York Dadaists. In protest Duchamp resigned from the board of the Independent Artists.

Rejection and notoriety only helped to increase Duchamp's fame. Fountain is regarded by many as a major landmark of twentieth century art. Duchamp's fame increased in time. He was consulted by such art moguls as Peggy Guggenheim on her modern art collection and shows. Duchamp, thus, helped shape the taste of Western art collectors and consumers in more than one way. A modern art award, The Marcel Duchamp Prize, is named after him in France. Duchamp, upon his return to Paris in 1923, devoted the rest of his life to studying chess, to the exclusion of most of his artistic endeavors. He earned the title of chess master and played in the French Championships and the Chess Olympiad.

Duchamp's Fountain was named the most influential modern artwork of all time. Fountain came top of a poll of 500 art experts, in the run-up to 2004 Turner Prize, above such names as Picasso, Cézanne, Matisse, and Warhol. The Turner Prize, named after the English painter J. M. W. Turner (1775-1851), is an annual prize presented to a British visual artist under the age of 50.

Since its beginnings in 1984 the Turner prize has become Britain's most controversial art award, mainly due to such works as Damien Hirst's Mother and Child, Divided, a sculpture comprised of a bisected cow and calf, and Tracey Emin's unmade bed, imaginatively titled My Bed. Although painters and sculptors have also won the prize, it has become associated primarily with *conceptual art*.

The art world will never be the same after Duchamp. Conceptual art, that is, 'idea art' will become the dominant mode of artistic practice. However, it also marks the end of the 'progressive era' in art. Since the nineteenth century one style/school of art followed another – Impressionism, Pointillism, Fauvism, Suprematism, Dadaism, Futurism, Surrealism, Cubism, Minimalism, Abstract Expressionism, Conceptualism. The list goes on and on.

With Conceptualism, or Conceptual Art, the wheel of progress in art seems to have ground to a perpetual halt. In the words of Danto, after Duchamp and his conceptual stratagems 'Everything is possible. Anything can be art'. Duchamp's posture necessitated posing the question 'What is art?' There seems to be no grander or more significant question to ask or a gesture to make for artists after it. After Duchamp, no innovation in art seemed to be possible.

From a Hegelian perspective Danto argues that with conceptualism art has reached its ultimate teleological goal of self-realization. As Hegel's Geist seeks self-fulfillment and realization by reaching complete self-understanding, art, by asking 'what is art?', completes its ultimate goal of self-understanding and becomes a sort of philosophical or theoretical investigation of the nature of art, nullifying the need for its original purpose. With conceptual art, art has become a sort of visual philosophy.

Conceptual Art

In a general sense, conceptual art is any work of art which gives primacy to the 'ideational content' or the idea behind the work over its formal aspects. Sometimes called 'concept art' or 'idea art', it was the leading art movement of the 60s and 70s. Its influence is still felt strongly in contemporary art.

Conceptual artists eschewed use of traditional materials such as paint or charcoal in their works. The dictum of Conceptual Art is 'art as idea'. It is based on the idea of separation of thinking from doing. In this respect it is a perfect art for the computer age. Computing is based on the divorce of cognitive skills from physical ones (see the figure below). Think of a musician. A musician since the advent of the home computer can, and does, compose a song and record it on a computer without physically hitting a single note. The music technology certainly helps free the creative mind from its physical limitations.

Computer Automation

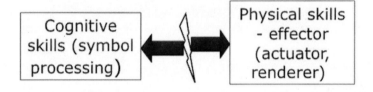

Computers as symbol processors – separation of mental processes from physical realization.

In a similar fashion, conceptual artists create art often without getting their hands dirty with paint or mud. The essential issue for conceptual art is the separation of art (idea or software) from its material embodiment (hardware), and the preferred media for conceptual art has often been found objects, language, or graphics.

Conceptual art de-emphasizes the value traditionally accorded to the materiality of art objects. The art object in conceptual art is not materially but conceptually defined, and its importance is located almost exclusively in its meaning. It focuses on examining the preconditions for the emergence of meaning in art, which is seen as a semiotic system, that is, a kind of language. Conceptual art in fact follows the trend of eliminating one-by-one the elements that make up artistic mastery set up by the original mechanization of art with the invention of photography:

$$\text{mind} + \text{eye} + \text{hand} = \text{art/craft} - \text{hand} = \text{photography} - \text{eye}$$
$$= \text{idea art}$$

The hand and the eye may have been made redundant, at least partially, in conceptual art, but fortunately artists continue to possess artisanal skills that they seem to hold back from bestowing on their works.

Conceptual Art as Popular Text

Works of conceptual art can be compared to works of popular culture. Like popular texts, most contemporary works of conceptual art are minimally crafted, simple, incomplete, full of gaps and insufficient in themselves. One of the leading figures of the Conceptual Art movement, Sol LeWitt, wrote that 'In conceptual art, the idea or concept is the most important aspect of the work... *The idea need not be complex*. Most ideas that are successful are ludicrously simple.'[31] Tracey Emin's My Bed is a concrete vindication of the above claim by LeWitt

French art critic and curator Nicolas Bourriaud characterizes the art of the 1990s, which is also applicable to today's art, as a culture of *use* and *do-it-yourself*, and the effacement of the boundary between art and everyday life:

Nowadays modernity extends into the practices of cultural do-it yourself and recycling, into the invention of the *everyday* and the development of time lived, which are not objects less deserving attention and examination than Messianistic utopias and the normal 'novelties' that typified modernity yesterday.[32]

According to Bourriaud contemporary art gains meaning with the active participation, as in popular works, of the viewer, unlike 'highbrow art' which invites passive contemplation. The same idea is expressed by Duchamp in the following words:

> The creative act is not performed by the artist alone; the spectator brings the work in contact with the external world by deciphering and interpreting its inner qualifications and thus adds his contribution to the creative act.[33]

The point is apparently well taken by Yuan Chai and Jian Jun Xi, two performance artists, who jumped on My Bed – rather, the bed of Tracey Emin – naked during its Tate Gallery showing in order to 'improve' the work. They called their 'work' Two Naked Men Jump Into Tracey's Bed. As part of their 'performance', the two men also had a pillow fight on the bed to a rousing round of applause from the gallery visitors, before being removed by security guards.

There is, however, at least one fundamental difference that differentiates works of popular culture from varieties of conceptual art. The former is marked and characterized by the social class, gender, and racial affiliations and differences of the people who create them, and make sense in such contexts, whereas the latter, generally speaking, are not marked by such differences. This may well be at the root of unpopularity and lack of social impact/relevance of much of contemporary art. Contemporary art is *like* popular text but without a populace or *people*, in whose everyday life contexts the work is produced, and gains its value and meaning. Without a social group or community within which to firmly ground it, most contemporary art withers into insignificance.

The small inventions of contemporary conceptual art are so contrived and removed, on the whole, from the lives of ordinary people that they look dull and dim witted compared to real works of popular culture. In general, amateur works of popular culture created by ordinary people as part of their everyday lives outshine their professional counterparts.

Luckily, there is an emerging strand of conceptual art which takes another route to invention. Instead of imitating life, that is, what popular culture produces, it delves into scientific ideas and research to create something out of ordinary.

Let's take a quick quiz from the book *Information Arts: Intersections of Art, Science, and Technology* by Steve Wilson.[34] Try to guess which of the following works are by artists and which are by scientists:

- Researcher J.T. developed a method of using genetic engineering to encode messages in bacteria.
- Researcher S. developed an arrangement so that a person far away could control his body through electrical stimulation.
- Researchers C.E. and U.W. bred a line of mice with a special proclivity for eating computer cables.
- Researcher P.D. developed a method for modulating sound onto the flow of dripping water.
- Researchers at M.R. developed a device that is sensitive to hugs and can react to things it hears on television.[35]

Information Arts

Information art is a relatively new term applied to a particular kind of conceptual art that mingles art with science and technology. The meaning and character of science and technology oriented art has been changing dramatically since the beginning of the 1990s. Artists that experiment with science and technology in recent years do not see art, as their predecessors in the 60s and 70s, as a practice of creating merely aesthetic objects or social commentary. Instead, art has become a kind of *basic research* that scientists undertake to understand the world.

The experimental and conceptual art of the 60s and 70s was influenced by the techno-scientific discourse dominant in that period. The questions these artworks raised were in general limited to cybernetics and related discourses of systems science, and information technology. In the new *information arts* a diverse range of disciplines contribute directly to the creation of artworks, such as biology, genetic engineering, space science and astronomy, nanotechnology, communication and information technologies, artificial intelligence, and materials science. This marks a shift from 'art as concept' or conceptual art to 'art as fully developed research document' or information art.[36]

Mingling of art and science is not something completely original. In the beginning, science and art were one. This was the case up until the nineteenth century. Leonardo da Vinci, the prototypical Renaissance man, is a well-known case of an artist who also excelled in science and engineering. Nevertheless, after at least a century of separation from science, art is becoming once again a sophisticated form of research-based work that takes part in knowledge production directly or indirectly. In this transformation, a shift from the work of art as representation of ideas or opinions of its creator(s) to the work of art as representation of fully worked-out research problems can be observed. In some cases, the work of art requires invention of new tools or devices that could potentially be useful for scientific research. In other cases, the work of art embodies ideas that could inspire scientists to see in a new light, or think differently about, the fundamental principles in their fields, and in this way contribute directly to scientific thinking and research.

An example from *bioarts*, currently an intensive area of artistic activity, would illustrate how art could contribute to innovation and radical new ways of thinking in science. In his 1990 work *Microvenus*, Joe Davis digitized and translated a figure based on Germanic rune, *algiz*, representing the female Earth, into a string of 28 DNA nucleotides. The genetically engineered DNA sequences that carry the graphical message were then inserted into the genomes of living E. coli bacteria. Davis called this work an 'infogene'. Twenty or so years ago Davis' idea of using DNA to encode extra-biological information, not just genetic sequences, was novel and did not have many precedents. Today, computer scientists and genetic engineers are working on DNA computing technologies and biological computers that could revolutionize computer science in the not too distant future.

The importance of Microvenus is that it has the *potential* to inform or inspire those with the relevant background and preparedness to think radically about fundamentals of computer science. It, therefore, illustrates how artistic creativity could be a source of inspiration and perhaps potential knowledge, and could have significant consequences for scientific research.

Another work of interest is Alba, the green fluorescent bunny. Alba is an albino rabbit. This means that, since she has no skin pigment, under ordinary environmental conditions she is completely white with pink eyes. However, when illuminated with the correct light (blue light maximum excitation at 488nm), she glows bright green. She is created by a contemporary artist Eduardo Kac by modifying her DNA with a green fluorescent gene found in the jellyfish Aequorea Victoria. 'Enhanced' with the new gene Alba shines under the right conditions. The significance of Alba lies not so much in its potential for contributing to the knowledge stock of genetic engineering as its symbolic value as an icon of the so-called 'information society'.

Pure Culture by Phil Ross is another example of the new kind of works that combine art and science:

Pure culture is a project in which I have been growing a series of sculptural objects from living mushrooms. ...This one was grown to take on the form of Harold Edgerton's famous photograph of a drop of milk splashing into some water. It was exhibited while alive in a sealed vitrine.[37]

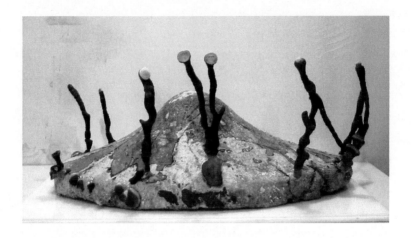

From the *Pure Culture* series. Phil Ross, 2000. Ganoderma lucidum fungus. Image courtesy of the artist.

Art or Science

Information arts seem to offer a way out of the current predicament of contemporary art. Instead of being an insignificant side note in people's lives, it aspires to the glories of scientific heights.

Interestingly, Duchamp himself engaged in artscience experiments. During his tenure in the Bibliotèque Sainte-Geneviève as a librarian he developed an interest in mathematics and physics, especially in the work of Jules Henri Poincaré (1854-1912). Poincaré was a polymath who made fundamental contributions to applied mathematics, physics, and mechanics. He is credited, in particular, for the theory of special relativity that he developed independently of Einstein, and the discovery of chaotic deterministic systems that laid the foundations of modern chaos theory.

In his 3 Standard Stoppages (*3 Stoppages Étalon*), Duchamp created an artwork by dropping three one-meter long threads from a height of one meter, onto three canvases. Each individual thread was then fixed on the exact position it fell on the canvas. The three canvases were then cut and stuck onto glass plates along with wooden rulers that were cut following the same curves of the threads. They were then encased in a wooden box. The work seems to be influenced by Poincaré's work on chance and determinism. In particular, the ideas in this work seems to be derived from the discussion of classical mechanics in a section entitled 'The Thread School' in Poincaré's book *Science and Hypothesis.*

It is generally accepted that art depends on the current mode of thinking, or the dominant paradigm in science. According to famous Italian novelist, medievalist, semiotician and philosopher Umberto Eco, best known for his novel *The Name of the Rose*, 'at any given moment in history, art is conceptually tied to whatever the dominant scientific model of that time is.' But does science need art?

Art and Science

It is well known that the use of linear perspective in Renaissance painting, which was first demonstrated in around 1413 by Filippo Brunelleschi, a Renaissance engineer and architect from Florence, and perfected by Leonardo da Vinci in the sixteenth century, mirrored the development of the knowledge in optics between the eleventh and seventeenth centuries.

In the early eleventh century, Ibn al-Haytham (965-1040), a Muslim physicist and polymath, wrote a book on optics. This work provided the first correct explanation of vision, which influenced the development of the modern telescope.

Around 1284 Salvino D'Armate of Florence invented the first wearable eyeglasses. The first rudimentary telescopes were developed independently in the sixteenth century by Giambattista della Porta, an Italian scholar and playwright, Taqi al-Din, an Ottoman scientist and polymath, and Leonard Digges, an English mathematician and surveyor.

The earliest known working telescopes were developed in the Netherlands in 1608. In the following year, Galileo Galilei improved upon these designs, and used a telescope to observe the sky. His observations confirmed the *heliocentric* model of the solar system, that is, the Earth and planets revolving around the Sun, which was developed by Nicolaus Copernicus, changing our understanding of the universe in a fundamental way. In 1668, Isaac Newton constructed the first practical reflecting telescope. In 1704 Newton published what is considered one of the great works of science in history, *Opticks*.

In *Secret Knowledge: Rediscovering the Lost Techniques of the Old Masters*,[38] British artist David Hockney (1937-) argues that optical devices and techniques were used in many of the masterpieces of the Old Masters of the Renaissance and post-Renaissance, such as Jan Van Eyck and Caravaggio. Among the optical devices claimed to be used are *camera obscura, camera lucida,* and curved mirrors, which allowed the image of the subject to be projected onto the surface of the canvas.

Hockney's work was a result of his collaboration with an American physicist and an expert on the optical properties of thin film Charles Falco (1948-) who argued that the use of optical aids by Renaissance artists might have been initiated as a result of Ibn al-Haytham's work on optics.

The Hockney-Falco thesis has attracted many criticisms. For instance, the Art Renewal Center, an organization led by millionaire businessman and art collector Fred Ross 'dedicated to the promotion classical realism in art as opposed to the Modernist developments of the twentieth century', claims that the existence of contemporary artists who produce photorealistic works without the use of optical aids disprove the Hockney-Falco thesis.

There are many other posited parallels between developments in scientific knowledge and art. İsmail Tunalı, a Turkish philosopher of art, argues that *impressionism* in art mirrors Austrian physicist and philosopher Ernst Mach's (1838-1916) theories on the physics of sound and light and his philosophy of radical empiricism. Tunalı argues similarly that *abstract* (non-figurative) *art* reflects developments in the quantum theory of light developed by German physicist Max Planck (1858-1947), and Einstein's theory of relativity.[39]

It should be clear from this brief discussion that art movements and innovations are closely tied to the developments in science and technology. But is the reverse true? Why, as I have argued above, has art become a kind of research activity in recent years? These questions still call for an answer.

Artscience: Theory Lock-in

Scientific practice is often locked in a certain theory or paradigm. A *paradigm*, or a way of looking at things, is essentially a set of principles that prescribe what is acceptable and unacceptable as theory in a scientific discipline. For instance, in *epidemiology*, that is the study of incidence and distribution of diseases in a population, there are two main competing approaches or paradigms: the dominant biomedical paradigm, and alternative emerging socially oriented paradigms. The dominant biomedical paradigm focuses on the biology of disease. It is criticized for ignoring the contextual factors, such as the level of social and economic development of a given society. The alternative paradigms in epidemiology prioritize general socio-economic and environmental factors in combating diseases and improving public health.

Thomas S. Kuhn's (1922-1996) seminal work on the history of science shows that there is normally a single central paradigm, a single way of doing science in established fields such as physics and astronomy, which he called 'normal science'. However, before the establishment of a central paradigm in a field, there is a period of what Kuhn called 'prescience', which is characterized by the existence of two or more alternative frameworks that compete to become the central paradigm, as in the case of the dominant and alternative paradigms in epidemiology.

Similarly, at the moments of crises in 'normal science', that is, when the central paradigm could no longer accommodate accumulating contradictory and conflicting results and observations, a number of alternative explanations of the anomalies compete. This is a period of 'revolutionary science' according to Kuhn. When a new theory successfully resolves the anomalies, a 'paradigm shift' happens, i.e. the old paradigm is replaced by the new, as in the case of relativity and quantum theories replacing Newton's physics.

Arguably, there is a general crisis in science today. The 'end of science' is a serious topic debated among scientists and philosophers of science alike. John Horgan's provocative book *The End of Science: Facing the Limits of Knowledge in the Twilight of the Scientific Age*,[40] published in 1996, contains opinions of many leading scientists in neurology, cognitive science, physics, biology, etc., who believe that the progress in pure science (of the kind made by Galileo, Newton, Darwin, Einstein) may be coming to an end. Although the book is not generally well received by the scientific community, and criticized for being postmodern, wishy-washy and fundamentally wrong in its arguments, it does raise interesting questions on the nature and future of 'Big Science'.

Science might end, not because of some postmodern skeptics who question and ridicule the validity and value of the scientific approach, but because, as Horgan argues, we might have reached the limit of knowing everything that is capable of being known, and/or the point where new ideas about the universe, such as *string theory*, are too difficult to experimentally test and falsify. Perhaps a better argument would be, not that science is ending as such, but that the *current set of paradigms* might be coming to an end in the Kuhnian sense.

Most of the last major breakthroughs in science, which paved the way for the ontological shift from 'stillness to motion as the natural state of the physical world' in the words of Newman and Holzman in their book *The End of Knowing*, took place in the period between the first half of the nineteenth century and the first half of the twentieth. Evolution theory of the species, quantum theory of light and matter, special and general relativity theories of time and space, cybernetics or the science of control in animals and machines, information theory of coding data for telecommunication, chaos theory, the double-helix model of DNA structure, and the first digital computer, have all been developed during this period, which provided us with a new ontology, a fresh view of nature and reality. This new reality is based on the model of chaotic dynamics of destruction and creation, and unpredictability, which stands in contrast to the classical paradigm of science that preceded it.

The classical paradigm, which is also known alternately as the Cartesian or Newtonian worldview, emerged in the sixteenth and seventeenth centuries. The Newtonian paradigm posits a mechanistic view of the universe. The main characteristics of this universe were that the world is a deterministic machine that could be completely understood by analyzing it in terms of its constituent parts. Events in this universe are analyzed in terms of linear cause and effect chains, and the observed phenomena are assumed to be completely isolated from the observers of the phenomena. In this universe of linear causality, there is no place for uncertainty, chance, or creativity. In short, it was based on the model of the mechanical clockwork, which is totally determined, predictable, and thus for all practical purposes in perpetual stillness.

The archetypal manifestation of the classical mechanistic view of the world in visual arts is the use of linear perspective in Renaissance painting, which was perfected by Leonardo da Vinci, as we briefly saw earlier.

One of the revolutions in the scientific outlook brought about by quantum physics is the discovery of the inherent duality in nature. Quantum physics has shown the inadequacy of the classical conception of subatomic entities as particles. In a series of well-known experiments at the turn of the last century, physicists discovered that so-called quantum 'objects' exhibit properties of both waves and particles. Quantum physics suggests that at the atomic level it makes better sense to talk about network of relations among wave-particles that extend in space-time, rather than isolated or locally determined particles. This property of nature is sometimes known as *quantum non-locality*. The paradox of *quantum entanglement* is a manifestation of this property of nature, where two 'particles' non-collocated, nonetheless, are causally linked, such that a change on the quantum state of one particle instantaneously affects the quantum state of the other particle, defying the law enshrined by Einstein's special relativity theory that distant particles cannot interact faster than the speed of light.

The paradigmatic shift in the contemporary scientific Weltanschauung, or worldview, has culminated in the dynamic view of the universe. The new worldview presents an evolving, changing, relational universe, where each particle is a part of a larger whole. In this universe of continuous change and exchange, interacting entities form dynamic loops of creation and destruction, defined in relation to each other, rather than the isolation of classical science's closed system model of nature.

The new relational view of nature is reflected in contemporary art. Art theorist Nicolas Bourriaud calls contemporary art 'Relational Art' and puts it in the context of related movements from art history: 'Relational aesthetics tries to decode or understand the type of relations to the viewer produced by the work of art. Minimalism addressed the question of the viewer's participation in phenomenological terms. The art of the 90s addresses it in terms of use.'[41]

It is arguable that an ontological shift, that is a shift in our views about the nature of reality, similar in scale to the transition from the Newtonian to relativistic and quantum worldviews, is highly unlikely to happen again, at least in the foreseeable future.

In other words, 'normal' science in the mold of physics or astronomy, with a single central paradigm, will increasingly be an exception and not the norm in the sciences of the future.

The latest conundrums such as quantum entanglement, and developments in the new 'Sciences of the Artificial', in the words of Herbert Simon[42] (1916-2001), such as chaos theory, complex dynamic systems, fractal geometry, as well as neuroscience, genetic engineering, and others suggest that the rationalist's ideal of the linear and smooth progress of science is no longer maintainable. It is highly plausible that the new sciences will not evolve into 'normal' science, but continue to exhibit the characteristics of what Kuhn called 'prescience' – a field of study with numerous competing paradigms without an overall winner or central paradigm.

Not only do the 'new sciences' pose challenges to the ideal of 'normal' science with a central explanatory paradigm. Theoretical physicists are yet to formulate a consistent theory that reconciles quantum mechanics with general relativity. The incompatibility of the two theories continues to be an insurmountable problem in physics. *String theory* and *loop quantum gravity* are two frameworks or paradigms that compete to provide an overarching theory. Similarly, the hope of a 'Grand Unified Theory' that unifies the strong, weak, electromagnetic, and gravitational forces into one single force continues to be an elusive idea in contemporary physics. Many such theories have been proposed, but none of them has gained general acceptance so far. The ideal of 'normal' science seems to escape modern physics too.

Another factor that contributes to the deviation from 'normal' science in particle physics is the difficulty of testing of some of the new theories. For instance, string theory has been criticized as *unscientific* because it is remarkably difficult to test experimentally. The difficulty in experimental testing of the string theory is mainly due to two reasons. Firstly, it requires extremely high energies, higher by order of magnitude than those needed in the recent experiments in the Large Hadron Collider at CERN. Secondly, it is not *falsifiable*, at least not in the way of conventional scientific theories. Famous Austrian-British philosopher of science Karl Popper (1902-1994) came up with the requirement that to be scientific a theory must be 'falsifiable'. That is, for a theory to be scientific, it must be possible to make predictions that depend on the distinct aspects of the theory such that if they are wrong the theory is wrong.

String theory in its current state of development entertains a great number of equally plausible models. Particular string theory models may be falsifiable, but the great variety of models make it very hard if not impossible in practice to come up with a viable test for the whole framework. These characteristics of the string theory cause it to have little or no predictive power. The great variety of competing models and the difficulty in experimentally testing them makes the string theory more of a 'prescience' than 'normal' science in a Kuhnian sense.

The current trend of deviation from the norms of the 'normal' science suggests that the new sciences, and arguably modern physics too, need a new way of legitimating themselves. According to Lyotard (1924-1998), a French postmodern philosopher, this takes the form of 'paralogy', or innovative ways of interpreting the world, invention of new ideas, 'little new narratives' or paradigms, if you will. This is precisely where the current interest in *artscience* experiments lies in my view. The idea *art*, as we have seen, is all about such little inventions. And although, as we have seen, most conceptual art did away to a large extent with the measuring eye and the crafting hand, today's artists, at least majority of them, thankfully still possess artisanal competencies that they hold back from bestowing on their works, but which are needed in order to transform the material reality and create something new out of it.

Whereas scientific invention is primarily epistemological,

artistic practice is primarily experiential, embodied and sensorial, that is, firstly ontological, only secondarily epistemological, even in the case of most conceptual art today.

The human aesthetic capacity that artists seem to entertain is related to living bodies' heightened sensitivity to discern meaningful distinctions between things, which is a prerequisite for creating something new. The human aesthetic capacity is intimately tied to our bodily affections and ability to engage with and transform physical materials.

Scientists are often locked in a certain theory or paradigm, a certain way of doing things, which may not be always conducive to paralogy, i.e. to the creation of little new narratives, new ways of seeing things. Technological and scientific innovations, especially radical ones, require intuition or pre-theoretical understanding; something which comes to most artists naturally. This is why in my view new sciences need artists more than ever. Symmetrically, artists, as we've seen, need progress in science, new ways of understanding the world, for artistic innovation and progress. Which perhaps explains science's happy new entanglement with art.

5

The Next Cycle: Onticapitalism

• **Wealth Of Nations: Macroeconomics Of Innovation** • **Model T** • **Making Of A Labor Sausage: Appropriation of Cultural Capital** • **Twenty First Century Schizoid Man** • **Pleasure Principle: Monkey See, Monkey Do** • **Sausages** • **Cars Again: Toyota Goes Post-Fordist** • **Re-Location: Toyota Losing Its Way** • **Pushing Wood, Paper, Information** • **Popular Economics: Glorimeters** • **On To Ontic-Capitalism**

Wealth of Nations: Macroeconomics of Innovation

It is the aim of the final chapter of the book to put innovation and social and cultural development in a wider context and point to future directions for new ways of living and working, that is, a new economy. The central thesis of this chapter is that innovation cannot be adequately studied at the micro-level of individual persons and companies; a wider societal and historical perspective is needed. This chapter aims to bring together the micro- and the macro- levels.

The unequal distribution of material wealth within society, or globally between nations, is a well-known fact. Both within society between different social groups, and between different nations of the world there is a wide gap in terms of concentration of money and material resources. However, symmetrical unequal distribution of skills and culture is generally overlooked and rarely gets the attention it deserves. I will argue below that invention and innovation are linked intimately to the attempts by the materially and/or culturally underdeveloped, be it individuals in a society or nations at an international scale, to catch up with the more advanced formations both at social and international levels.

The rise and fall of nations and empires, as well as companies, could be seen in this light: a *qualitative leap forward*, a *cultural coup* by the underdeveloped in a bid to catch up and overtake the more advanced. As we have seen, the gradual swing of wealth and power from the East to the West around the fifteenth century was largely due to technological innovations in navigation and discovery of new trade routes. The cultural consequences of the discoveries of the new trade routes and the 'new world' had been two-way, as discussed in Chapter 2: deskilling and ultimately decimation for the native cultures, and a tremendous leap forward in skills and technology for Europe.

The same set of innovations also marked, as we saw briefly in the same chapter, the rise of a new class, the bourgeoisie, and the invention of 'merchant capitalism'. The transfer of sovereignty from aristocracy to bourgeoisie was completed as merchant capitalism slowly evolved into 'industrial capitalism', which was made possible with such technological inventions as the steam engine, the Jacquard loom, and later on, the internal combustion engine, and the 'assembly line'. The latter two were responsible, of course, for the birth of the automobile, which we turn our attention to next.

With a twist of fate, since the invention of the Jacquard loom in 1801, and especially the twin inventions of 'scientific management' by Frederick Winslow Taylor and the 'assembly line' by Henry Ford around the turn of the twentieth century, capitalism has been responsible for the de-skilling of the very same people who helped in the making of capitalism and its gradual development with skilful use of technological, scientific, and cultural innovations made since the Age of Discovery.

Model T

Ford Model T was the first automobile mass-produced on the assembly line according to Frederick Winslow Taylor's (1856-1915) principles of 'scientific management'. Taylor was an

American mechanical engineer who, in a bid to lower the labor cost in the manufacturing process, broke down the manual tasks carried out by workers into micro movements in time and re-combined them to synthesize mechanical workflows to improve efficiency and increase productivity. The 'time and motion analysis' of human labor was the basis of the assembly line in which a set of optimally planned and standardized sequential motions were repeated to speed up the manufacturing process in orders of magnitude in comparison to handcrafting methods. Taylor wrote:

> All possible brainwork should be removed from the shop and centered in the planning or laying-out department. ... The work of every workman is planned out by the management at least one day in advance, and each man receives in most cases complete written instructions, describing the task in detail, which he is to accomplish. ... This task specifies not only what is to be done but how it is to be done and the exact time allowed for doing it.[43]

Henry Ford's (1863-1947) application of Taylorism to automobile manufacturing did not, however, go without considerable resis-tance from the work force. In *The Case for Working with Your Hands*[44] Matthew Crawford quotes from one of Ford's biogra-phers:

> So great was labor's dissatisfaction taste for the new machine system that toward the close of 1913 every time the company wanted to add 100 men to its factory personnel, it was necessary to hire 963.

Before the introduction of the assembly line automobiles were 'built' by workers recruited from bicycle and carriage shops. One such craftsman was George Sturt whose account of pre-assembly line days of automobile manufacturing is summarized as follows in Crawford's words:

> In Sturt's shop, working exclusively with hand tools, the skills required to build a wheel regress all the way to selection of trees to fell for timber, the proper time for felling them, how to season them, and so forth.

Crawford quotes a lengthy passage from Sturt's own book *Wheelwright's Shop* that illustrates the rich and rewarding world of the pre-assembly line craftsmen; a part of which is reproduced below:

> Yet it is in vain to go into details at this point; for when the simple apparatus had all be gotten together for one simple-looking process, a never-ending series of variations was introduced by the material. What though two felloes [a section of the wheel's rim] might seem look much alike when finished? It was the wheelwright himself who had to make them so. He it was who hewed out that resemblance from quite dissimilar blocks, for no two felloe-blocks were ever like. ... He had no band-saw (as now [1923]) to drive, with ruthless *unintelligence* [my emphasis], through every resistance. The timber was far from being prey, a helpless victim, to a machine. Rather it would lend its own special virtues to the man who knew how to humor it.

This was all to change with the application of the 'scientific management' principles to the manufacturing process by Henry Ford in around 1913, which has come to be known as Fordism:

- Standardization of the product
- Use of special-purpose tools and equipment via the assembly line

- Elimination of skilled labor in direct production
- Relocation of cognitive labor to the design, planning, and research & development departments

Fordism was, however, more than Taylorism plus factory automation. It comprised a whole new ideology centered-around mass production by means of mechanization of the manufacturing process and mass consumption by means of 'social engineering' or 'consumption engineering' of needs and wants. Fordism, thus, signaled the beginning of degradation of the 'blue-collar worker' and the birth of a new class – the 'white-collar worker'. Fordism came to connote in the public imagination the 'rationalization' of the work process and the birth of the 'machine civilization'.

Making of a Labor Sausage: Appropriation of Cultural Capital

The necessary cognitive and manual skills were undoubtedly considerable, even for a small job such as wheel building, before the application of scientific management to manufacturing. No wonder: it was difficult in the early days to recruit workers to the alienating world of Henry Ford's assembly line from the cognitively rich and rewarding world of bicycle and carriage shops of autonomous craftsmen.

Even relatively high wages offered by the new industries based on the assembly line were not enough to lure the craftsmen to the alienating world of factory automation. A clever way of overcoming worker resistance to the mechanization of skills had to be found, and it came, as Crawford points in his book, in the form of *consumer debt*. Before the turn of the twentieth century, being indebted would attract moral culpability. As Jackson Lears wrote in 'The American Way of Debt' in the *New York Times Magazine* (11 June 2006):

Indebtedness signified a sin against the Protestant ethic of self-control; it also threatened the ideal of independent manhood that underwrote the founders' vision of a virtuous republic. ... Benjamin Franklin coined ... aphorisms later memorized by generations of Victorian-era schoolchildren: 'The borrower is a slave to the lender.' 'Be frugal and free.'

[...]

After 1900, the proliferation of mass-marketed products encouraged a more open tolerance for consumer debt. By the 1920s, millions of middle-class Americans bought durable goods on time payments – sewing machines, washing machines, radios, automobiles, houses. Lenders acquired legitimacy, reinforced by reassuring names like Household Finance Corporation or General Motors Acceptance Corporation.

All this was in order to rob manual workers, craftsmen and artisans of their *cultural capital*, i.e. integrated sets of cognitive and manual skills and competencies. Let's read it from Lear's piece (emphasis mine):

Indebtedness could discipline workers, keeping them at *routinized* jobs in factories and offices, graying but in harness, meeting payments regularly. Good consumers would be good producers. The economist who proposed this idea was Simon Nelson Patten, in *The New Basis of Civilization* (1907). By providing new sanctions for spending, Patten helped create a cultural landscape where consumer debt could find a decent suburban home. He predicted that workers' desires for things would not undermine their capacity for disciplined achievement, as generations of moralists had claimed; rather, the multiplication of wants would become part of the *civilizing* process, as workingmen and their wives would broaden their horizons and take pride in their accumulating possessions.

Take note of the very last words above: 'accumulating posses-sions' implies counting, accounting, that is *quantification* of life. We will return to quantification of 'Being' below.

In sum, the end result of the 'rationalization' of human labor has been breaking-down of the artisanal skills and competencies into mechanical movements and their reconstitution in 'machine intelligence' of factory automation, or as Crawford aptly puts in his book, a 'labor sausage'.

Recently, grand but largely unrealized utopias of artificial intelligence and expert systems have aimed to extend the labor sausage outside of the factory floor into the offices of white-collar workers and hospital wards. Research in the sub-field of Artificial Intelligence, known as expert systems, aims to codify the know-how in human minds into rules and atomic statements; extending the studies of 'time and motion' of human physiology pioneered by Frederick Taylor to the studies of 'time and thought'. As Crawford points out, this is equivalent to transfer of knowledge, skills, and decision making from white-collar workers (engineers, doctors, nurses, etc.) to managers.

Should this approach prove to be successful in several domains of knowledge-intensive work, it would mean the expansion of Taylor's dream to even greater realms of human labor capacity – an instance of further separation of thinking from doing. The 'expert systems' approach provides another example of the process that I called in the first chapter *quantifi-cation* of *qualities* inherent in human labor capacity, or more simply, transformation of quality into quantity.

Not only the work process but the whole cultural ecology has been overturned by the twin forces of Taylorism and Fordism. Culture, says Raymond Williams (1921-1988), who is credited as the founder of the field of 'cultural studies', comprises both the ordinary/everyday and the creative sides of life:

We use the word culture in these two senses: to mean *a whole way of life* – the common meanings; to mean the arts and learning – the special processes of discovery and creative effort. Some writers reserve the word for one or other of these senses; I insist on both, and on the significance of their conjunction.[45]

As Williams underlines above, the conjunction of the two, the ordinary/everyday and the creative, comprises a unified cultural field. They are entangled; a change in one never fails to trigger changes on the other. Demise of the skilled, creative, qualitative work hence meant the demise of the quality of *everyday* life. As we have seen, habituation of the craftsperson to the assembly line required persistent exposure to the culture of consumerism and credit debt, which in a vicious circle necessitated production of even greater quantities of goods in reduced costs, i.e. mass production.

To put it more succinctly, quantification/commercialization of everyday life and of work goes hand-in-hand. Without the one the other would not be possible. As Crawford points out 'Evidently, it [the assembly line] inspires revulsion only if one is acquainted with more satisfying modes of work'. We should add to the above statement '... if one is acquainted with more satisfying modes of work *and life.*'

Twenty First Century Schizoid Man[46]

A few years after the introduction of the assembly-line, the 7632 wagon and carriage manufacturers that had existed in 1900 were reduced to just three big ones as Fordism took America by storm, and consumerism and instant gratification came to replace a fuller social, cultural and psychological life.

A few of the 500 plus vehicles that took part in 60 mile 2011 Veteran Car Run from London to Brighton. (Image: Murat Karamuftuoglu).

The concentration of material and cultural capital in the hands of progressively fewer and fewer elites means the degradation of the quality of life for the majority, even though we have somewhat paradoxically come to believe that the 'standard' of life is on the increase on the whole for the whole of the planet. I will not discuss here the social and psychological problems that have been amplified since the advent of modern times, nor whether or not we *enjoy* a better *quality* of life compared to, say, the Middle Ages in the West or the East. Instead, I point the reader, in the true spirit of the book, to popular art to judge for themselves the quality of life in the twenty-first century. What counts is the *perceived* quality of life by the populace; after all, it will be the populace who will or will not make a cultural *coup d'état* to change the state of affairs.

Pleasure Principle: Monkey See, Monkey Do[47]

The answer to the paradoxical belief that the quality of life is on the increase is hidden, I think, in the statement quoted from Crawford earlier: 'evidently, it inspires revulsion only if one is acquainted with more satisfying modes of work [and life]'. Fast-food and instant gratification by consuming more of everything only repels if one's body and mind have been detoxified from culinary and cultural junk.

Anyone who had a chance to carefully observe a human offspring's physiological and psychological development would testify that our biological and psychic make-up is open to all sorts of manipulations. Helpless when born, we yearn for belonging and acceptance. We learn by imitation and trial and error, rather than thoughtful study. We are not particularly good at foresight, nor prudent when it comes to our long-term wellbeing, individually or collectively. Neither are we good at deferring gratification and cultivating our pleasures, despite the thousand-year-old wisdom of Taoist sex manuals. We easily get attached to our comforting habits and get intoxicated by them.

The biological, evolutionary, and social basis of the human psychic apparatuses and decision-making processes is a vast field of scientific study. The whole new emerging disciplines of 'neuroeconomics' and 'neuromarketing' attempt to combine psychology, economics and neuroscience to understand how humans categorize risks and rewards in decision-making, and exploit this for commercial gain. The pleasure principle, i.e. the instinctual impulse of seeking pleasure and avoiding pain that rules our early life, makes us easy prey to exploitation in our later lives: junk food will continue to sell as well as sugar candy and eye candy.

A *cultural coup*, that is a qualitative leap forward by the masses who have been robbed of their cultural capital would therefore require claiming a *qualitatively* rich world, and an ontologically satisfying way of life. I will argue further below that this has become a historical necessity with the gradual shift in power from the West to the East – a part of the series of historical cycles of leveling of the global playing field. The sorts of innovations in technology and culture required by the coming shift in the historical cycle will be treated in the concluding sections of this final chapter of the book. But first, anyone for sausages...?

Sausages

Everyone likes sausage, or most people do. Like sugar candy, sausage sells too. But this does not mean that life in the sausage factory needs to be intoxicating or alienating as in Ford's assembly-line factory. In *How I Learned to Let My Workers Lead*[48] Ralph Stayer, head of family-owned 'Johnsonville Sausage', gives an account of his personal experience of how, in search for improvements in the quality of his sausages, radically devolved the decision-making process from the managers to the shop-floor. The end-result was not only significant improvement in the quality of his sausages, but quality of life of his employees both inside and outside of the sausage factory, as well as the foundation of a kind of workplace democracy.

Stayer asked himself, do his employees 'work together like a strikingly synchronized flock of geese on the wing – sharing a goal, taking turns leading, and mastering the task at hand? Or do they seem more like a heard of buffalo – blindly following their leader and passively standing around waiting for instructions?'

According to Stayer his employees were 'bored, made dumb mistakes, and didn't care.' He states that:

> ...people saw nothing for themselves at Johnsonville. It was a job, a means to some end that lay outside the company. I wanted them to commit themselves to a company goal, but they saw little to commit to. ... I couldn't still see that the biggest obstacle to changing their point of view was me.
>
> [...]
>
> In fact, I expected my people to follow me the way buffalo follow their leader – blindly. Unfortunately, that kind of leadership model almost led to the buffalo's extinction.

Stayer realized in time that he had to change the whole decision-making process radically. The workers had to make decisions and control their own work: who is to hire, who is to fire, what sort of productivity and quality control measures should be put in place. It was all up to the workers in the new system. Lets hear it from Stayer:

> Teams had ... taken on responsibility for selecting, training, evaluating, and when necessary, terminating fellow employees. Now they began to make all decisions about schedules, performance standards, assignments, quality measures, and capital improvements as well. In operations, teams assumed the supervisors' functions and those jobs disappeared.
>
> [...]

I discovered that change occurs in fits and starts, and that while I could plan individual changes and events, I couldn't plan the whole process.

It was not easy to change the whole company culture by devolving the power structure. People initially refused to take responsibility and make their own decisions:

> I also discovered that in meetings people waited to hear my opinion before offering their own. ... I began to stay silent to avoid giving any clue to where I stood. The result that people flatly refused to commit themselves to any decisions at all.
>
> [...]
>
> In the end, I began scheduling myself out of many meetings, forcing others to make their decisions without me.

This 'post-Fordist' re-structuring of the work-life at Johnsonville Sausage had repercussions in other realms of workers' lives:

> We set up an educational allowance for each person, to be used however the individual saw fit. In the beginning, some took cooking or sewing classes; a few took flying lessons. Over time, however, more and more of the employees focused on job-related learning. Today more than 65% of all the people at Johnsonville are involved in some type of formal education. The end state we all now envision for Johnsonville is a company that never stops learning. One part of learning is the acquisition of facts and knowledge – about accounting, machine maintenance, marketing, even about sky diving and Italian cooking. But the most important kind of learning teaches us to question our own actions and behavior in order to better understand the ways we perform, work, and live. Helping human beings fulfill their potential is of course a moral responsibility but it's also good business. Life is

aspiration. Learning, striving people are happy people and good workers. They have initiative and imagination, and the companies they work for are rarely caught napping.

However, the real question is whether 'workplace democracy' could be extended to all realms of everyday life, a question to which we will return in the last few pages of the book.

Cars Again: Toyota Goes Post-Fordist[49]

Collapsing the walls between cognitive and manual work, flattening of the hierarchical power structures proved to be a good strategy in other companies too; we will now turn to the well-known case of Toyota.

The success of Toyota Motor Corporation and its reputation for reliability has been attributed to its innovative 'knowledge creation and management' techniques that are drawn largely from cultural traditions and dispositions of Japanese people for communal activity, the ability to exhibit sharing and empathy. The specific Japanese attitude to knowledge is sometimes expressed in connection to the concept of 'Ba', which could be understood as the 'dynamic unity of *space-time-people* that enables creation of an *atmosphere* or collective context in which knowledge is created, shared, and utilized through *informal* interaction', or simply 'embodied space/context for work'. *Ba* can encompass physical (office, factory floor, etc.), virtual (social media, teleconference, email), and mental (ideas, emotions, ideals) spheres of life, or any combination thereof.

In this conception, knowledge seems to be embedded in *Ba* – shared physical, virtual, and mental spaces. Knowledge in this sense is fundamentally 'tacit'; it is embedded in group practices and activities that incorporate individual skills and crafts. It is, therefore, hard to formalize or even verbalize. Nevertheless, when it is detached from *Ba* and externalized, it, or more accurately a part of it, can be turned into explicit rules and statements that can be communicated. Knowledge verbalized and transmitted by means of information and communication technologies becomes information.

The success of Toyota is attributed largely to its intimate understanding and appreciation of the value of collectively created tacit knowledge embedded in shared spaces. Whereas its Western competitors have traditionally attached importance to explicit knowledge, in other words, information, Toyota is known for its ability to harness the tacit knowledge of its employees. In contrast to Taylorism and Fordism, the so-called 'Toyota way' emphasizes the integration of cognitive and manual skills, and close cooperation between all parties of the production process, from the shop floor to internal research and development labs and external suppliers of components and parts. In fact, the remarkable agility showed by Toyota in recovering from a devastating fire in one of its main supplier's production plants was attributed to the close cooperation and collaboration between all parties of the production process.

On 1 February 1997, a fire in one of Toyota's top supplier's production facilities threatened to halt the entire Toyota production line for several weeks. The supplier in question was the sole source manufacturer of a crucial brake-related part used in all Toyota vehicles. Since both Toyota and its supplier was applying the 'Just-in-Time' production principle, there was only about two days' worth of stocks of the crucial part at hand and a complete shut-down of the entire production seemed inevitable; Toyota was facing the worst crisis in its corporate history to that date. However, after only three days of the fire, the consortium formed by some seventy of Toyota's partner firms, with no previous experience in manufacturing that particular brake-part, were manufacturing and delivering it to Toyota's assembly plants. How was this remarkable re-organization possible in such a short time?

The Toyota Way encourages and authorizes all line personnel

to stop the production line in case of an anomaly, and seek and find a solution that resolves it. This routine and continuous problem-solving practice, known as 'Kaizen', not only has been responsible for the incremental improvements in Toyota's production process over the years, but also provided the basis for the remarkable agility demonstrated by Toyota in the fire incident.

Academics Nishiguchi and Beaudet[50] who studied the incident reported that:

> ... with the cooperation of the union, the majority of employees were mobilized for the recovery effort which involved, for example, white-collar staff from advertising and accounting departments helping with plant operations. At Toyota the situation often dictated that managers and employees make decisions and take action on the spot without necessarily following normal procedures or obtaining permission from superiors or bookkeepers.

It was the culture of 'Kaizen', i.e. continuous improvement based on small experiments, and monitoring and adjustment of the production system based on the results of the small experiments, instead of large-scale pre-planning and extensive scheduling, as well as the 'Genchi Genbutsu' principle, which teaches that in order to truly understand a situation one needs to go the real place where the work is done and study the problem, which were at the heart of Toyota's agility and success. In the final analysis, the Toyota Way amounts to re-integration of cognitive and manual skills in the production line and flattening of the company-wide decision-making hierarchy. As one commentator observed:

> It is our conclusion that Toyota has developed a set of principles, Rules-in-Use we've called them, that allow organi-

zations to engage in this (self-reflective) design, testing, and improvement so that (nearly) *everyone can contribute at or near his or her potential, and when the parts come together the whole is much, much greater than the sum of the parts.*

[...]

We've seen that consistently – across functional roles, products, processes (assembly, equipment maintenance and repair, materials logistics, training, system redesign, administration, etc.), and hierarchical levels (from shop floor to plant manager and above) that in TPS [Toyota production System] managed organizations the design of nearly all work activities, connections among people, and pathways of connected activities over which products, services, and information take form are *specified-in-their-design, tested-with-their-every-use, and improved close in time, place, and person to the occurrence of every problem.*[51]

Re-location: Toyota Losing its Way

In view of such a remarkable success story and the firm reputation of Toyota for quality and reliability, how should one explain the recent recall disaster that hit the company, involving this time, ironically, the acceleration pedal? In three related episodes between 2009 and 2010 Toyota had to recall about eight million of its cars sold in North America, Europe and China.

Initially, Toyota designed and manufactured cars exclusively in Japan and exported them to markets abroad. This helped Toyota to have total control over its knowledge creation and management processes and culture. With the increase in demand and global drive for re-locating the manufacturing plants in countries where local labor costs are lower, Toyota has started to establish production bases in Asia and other regions. However, in its first wave of relocating its production bases Toyota stayed reliant on Japanese workers, designers and engineers in creating and managing new knowledge. In other words, the unity of mental and manual labor embedded in *Ba* gave way to separation of the two, specifically, research and design from manufacturing. Since 2004, Toyota has made a concentrated, albeit apparently not totally successful, effort to install similar knowledge creation and management systems in its plants abroad to tap into local customer, competitor and supplier knowledge. However, concerns voiced regarding the safety and quality of the new vehicles by the customers and local management were brushed aside. Global outsourcing and the difficulty of diffusing the Toyota Way to its new production bases in foreign soils and cultures, as well as aggressive cost-cutting exercises, appear to be at the root of the quality and safety issues that have afflicted Toyota Motor company lately.

The main moral of this story for our purposes is that relocation of the workforce and global outsourcing were at the heart of the destruction of *Ba*, that is, the dynamic unity of *space-time-people*, and therefore, *breaking-down* of the unity of cognitive and manual skills, or knowledge work and physical work. Extraction of knowledge embedded in *Ba* and its communication as abstract instructions and rules are also at the heart of the ongoing global economic and financial crisis, at which we will now have a brief look.

Pushing Wood, Paper, Information

'Woodpusher' is a common expression for a chess player of limited skill. Playing chess at grandmaster level, in contrast to common belief, is not about following rules, or evaluating the position of each piece on the board one by one. It is estimated that master players can play at the rate of 5-10 seconds a move or faster without degradation in performance, which rules out the possibility of rule-following or piece-by-piece evaluation of the board. In one experiment reported by contemporary American philosopher Hubert Dreyfus, who was the author of the book *What Computers Still Can't Do: A Critique of Artificial Reason,*[52] and one of the first to challenge claims for the possibility of 'artificial intelligence' in the early 70s, it is shown that a chess master can play chess against another master level player at a rate of five seconds per move, while his analytical mind is almost completely occupied by adding random numbers thrown at him at the rate of about one per second. This experiment demonstrates that master players exhibit gestalt recognition skills, i.e. the ability to almost instantly distinguish between different configurations of the chessboard, in fact, roughly 50,000 of them.[53] Doing without theorizing that I emphasized in the earlier chapters should be understood in the above sense of gestalt perception and action without rule-following.

Gestalt is a German word for 'organic form', used to denote a physical, biological, psychological, or symbolic configuration, a *whole*, which is irreducible and *more* than the sum of its constituent parts. Gestalt perception, therefore, involves *recognizing the whole at once*, without analyzing the individual elements that constitute it.

According to Maurice Merleau-Ponty (1908-1961), a French philosopher who rejected the separation of mind and body, everyday, absorbed, skilled acting, or simply 'skillful coping', is guided by the *preconscious* drive of the physical body to form a meaningful gestalt or organic whole with its environment. Experts, master craftsmen, indeed anyone engaged in skillful acting, experiences the performed activity as an uninterrupted transparent 'flow of movement' in response to one's perception of the situation/environment. Only at the point of *breaking-down* is the transparency lost and rules and conscious thinking are needed; much in the vein of Heidegger's account of the broken hammer given in Chapter 3.

I will argue below that what is true for an individual and her everyday skilful coping, or Being-in-the-World, is true on a grander scale for a whole society and its economic activities.

In a moment of revelation Newman and Holzman describe the

US economy, in contrast the general belief, as a *'regulatory* free market'. According to Newman and Holzman, in the wake of the great depression that lasted from 1929 until the late 1930s, 'regulatory-ism' emerged as the favored solution to the crisis of free market capitalism. In the post-depression years 'total trans-formation of the state and all its governmental arms from a loose *coordinating* agency to a highly centralized *regulatory* agency' had taken place. Newman and Holzman state that:

> Everything – banking, the market, business, science, education, labor, the poor (and everything in between) – has become increasingly regulated this past half century to control against future collapse(s) ...
>
> The regulated has, in turn, changed the very nature of US economics and politics ... For in a highly regulated market system (as opposed to a largely unregulated free market system), profitability ... is increasingly determined by who controls and best manipulates the regulations.

Please continue to read from Newman and Holzman, keeping in mind that the book was written in 1997, way before the current economic crisis:

> In *Tales of a New America* (1987), Robert Reich ... speaks of the dramatic transformation in the composition of corporate boards over the past fifty years; having been made up primarily of production and manufacturing related people. They are now more and more populated by lawyers (who know how to manipulate the regulations). ... With the erosion of the US manufacturing base, the 'manipulation of paper' (money, stocks, bonds) became the preferred area of economic growth [hence, the current so called 'credit crunch']; the regulated economy became a credit economy and, lawfully, a debt economy; the higher paid workforce became smaller and

more middle class (white collar). The US went from being the world's leading creditor nation [and biggest manufacturing base] to the world's largest debtor nation (in recent years Japan [and more recently China and India], in particular, taking advantage of America's regulatory-ism).

[...]

Highly regulated capitalism and the ever-increasing capacity to derive greater and greater profits from legal manipulations of regulations ... profoundly transformed the complex historical relationship between the political and the economic in the US society.

To translate it to Merleau-Ponty's or Heidegger's way of thinking, the *breaking-down* of the manufacturing base of the US economy (due to such neo-liberal management practices as *production offshoring, outsourcing* etc.), in other words, destruction of the gestalt of the economic life, foregrounded 'rules and regulations', in other words 'information and data flows' used in the 'command and control' of both legal and technical operations, as the basis of economic activity and growth in the US.

Not only lawyers, but technologists, especially those who work with information and telecommunication systems have immensely benefitted from the separation of thinking and doing at the global scale. Widespread use of information and telecom-munication technologies in turn accelerated and consolidated the fracturing of the immanent unity and immediacy of the *space-time-people* continuum. Economic growth based on pushing paper and information, manipulation of legal regulations and opera-tional technical data, instead of manufacturing things, proved to be *virtual* in light of the recent implosion of the *regulatory-ism* of the global finance/credit economy, confirming the foresight of Newman and Holzman from 1997.

We have seen in the case of Toyota that destruction of *Ba*, or the dynamic unity of *space-time-people*, was the main reason for deterioration in quality and ensuing technical difficulties and faults. Quality is a product of organic unity of mind and body, cognitive and manual skills. It should be, therefore, not simply understood as a product of handcrafting. Even in handcrafting, tools of varying degrees of complexity are used. The important point in this respect is the unity or gestalt of cognitive and manual labor rather than the use or not of specific tools in production.

With the destruction of *Ba* the unity of cognitive and manual labor was disrupted in Toyota Motor Cooperation. However, at the macro-level of the whole country, Japan's economic life has not suffered as badly, since unlike the US a strong manufacturing base continues to exist there, despite production offshoring and such by individual companies like Toyota.

Popular Economics: Glorimeters

We are physical creatures with bodies, that is, we are embodied. Our bodies play a fundamental and irreducible part in our being in the world, in our cognition, emotions, and psychological make-up. The cognitive and physical skills we acquire depend on our bodily existence in the physical world. This line of thinking is well rooted in Eastern thought, but largely suppressed in the West with the exception of perhaps Aristotle. In Western philosophy it was Henri Bergson (1859-1942) and Martin Heidegger (1889-1976) who broke off, independently of each other and in their own ways, from the Western tradition of separation of the mind and body that started with Plato and continued with Descartes. Merleau-Ponty, a follower of Heidegger, also contributed significantly to our understanding of the importance of body in the acquisition cognitive and physical skills.

Being embodied beings, we populate the physical world with our bodies, chairs, hammers, cars, sausages, computers, cloths, glasses, houses, bath tubs, TV sets, musical instruments, cups and plates, and so on and so forth. Similarly, we populate the virtual world of the internet, the greatest social medium invented so far, with emails and documents, and representations of ourselves, known as avatars, and the relationships or connections of various kinds between them. We will continue to need chairs and cups as well as online representations and mediations.

Manufacturing industries, therefore, will continue to be an essential part of any healthy society and economic organization, despite all the hype about post-industrial society and knowledge economies. As long as we are not completely done with our physical bodies we will require physical skills to cope with the ever-changing external world and populate it with other things and bodies.

By acting, by making mistakes, and learning from the mistakes, in short by learning by doing, one finally becomes an *autonomous* person, a person of 'practical wisdom'. In Aristotle's words, 'a person who does the appropriate thing at the appropriate time in an appropriate way.' That's *mastery*, which Heidegger thought the highest thing one could aspire to. By skillful everyday action and perception one can master the life on earth, and become an autonomous and wholesome person that leads an 'authentic' life.

Heidegger goes on to suggest that by mastering the art of *skillful coping* one can change the world by responding to a given situation in a way that changes people's perceptions of the situation – a truly poetic undertaking. There is a highly recommended short video on YouTube by Hubert Dreyfus on 'Embodiment', where he explains in simple terms the ideas of Heidegger and Merleau-Ponty summarized here.

The implausibility of the separation of thinking from doing in light of the above arguments also implies the implausibility and undesirability of social division of work into separate, mutually exclusive domains of intellectual and manual, scientific and artistic, managerial and technical, blue-collar and white-collar, and so on. That would make a post-capitalist organization of work and life as Karl Marx predicted it.

In such a world, economic performance would be evaluated not by productivity and profitability but by the skills, both cognitive and manual, imparted in the things that are created to populate our world. Personal happiness would be found not in the cash made or the number of things owned, but in one's life-long accumulated skills, and the skilful and creative use of the possibilities offered by the 'ready-to-hand' things that exist in the world in creating our own personal meanings relevant to our own everyday experiences. We will return to this further below, but first lets go back to Gabriel Tarde, the sociologist who analyzed society in terms of psychological interactions between individuals through the dual forces of imitation and invention.

Tarde suggested that money is an excellent measure of material wealth, but it misses all sorts of other *kinds* of valuations. According to Tarde the fact that wealth is much simpler and easier to measure has overshadowed all kinds of other valuations of one's social standing. In his generalized economics Tarde is for all kinds of valuations, fame, popularity, reputation, authority, etc.:

> How is a man's credit, his fame and his glory, born, and how does it grow in all of its forms? It is indeed worth looking at these different forms of production, as well as the production of wealth and of its venal value. ... If there are any 'natural laws' that regulate the manufacture of these or other items in greater or lesser quantities and the increase and decrease of their venal value, why would there not be one that would regulate the appearance, growth, increase or decrease of the popular enthusiasm for this or that man, or the royalist loyalty of a people, of its religious faith, of its trust in this or that institution?[54]

Money is too crude a measure for valuation of all sorts of passionate intensities in different spheres and multiplicities of life. What are needed are all sorts of new 'glorimeters', as Tarde calls them, to capture the popular standings in different realms of everyday life. Popular culture with its subcultures, fan sites and fanzines, is a testimony for such valuations. Opinion polls, marketing surveys, auctions in the worlds of marketing and politics, peer reviewing in academia, and new forms of measurements on the internet such as search engine rankings, links between web pages, number of downloads, and mouse clicks and so on and so forth, are all examples of valuations which in the final analysis tend to be reduced to the ubiquitous monetary form.

In the spirit of Tarde's generalized economics and the Johnsonville sausage factory, one could dream to extend valuations and meritocracy to all sorts of mundane economic activities and actors, from grocery shops to milkmen, and all sorts of innovations, from verbal and mental to physical and technical. Would it not be plausible to think of *glorimeters* or *valuemeters* that directly, without reducing them to monetary value, measure the popular standing, inventiveness, authority, trustworthiness, aesthetic qualities, and so on, of activities and work of foremen or postmen, tea ladies or secretaries, as well as the mighty and the famous, and the popular pleasures derived from them?

What we are suggesting here is doing away with money for a moment to imagine new kinds of glorimeters that give more sensitive and accurate readings of the multiplicity of popular activities. Popular culture is full of them, but Tarde's originality is his insistence that all sorts of passions, enthusiasms, and intensities are ready to hand for quantification without being reduced to cash flows, in other words, glorimeters that return numeric values for popular intensities, activities and inventions – a sort of a compromise solution that substitutes multiplicity of quantifications for simple cash flows.

Tarde was also acutely aware of the intensities registered by organized groups of people such as trade unions, and professional and voluntary associations; the kinds of activities that are usually underrepresented in popular culture studies. The bottom-up character of subcultures is commendable, however, there are realms of everyday life where top-down organization takes precedence over spontaneous action. Arguably, *popular democracy* becomes a plausible dream once *glorimeters* of all kinds register *directly*, bypassing the monetary form, measurements of passionate activities and innovations of people at work, school, parliament, the media and the rest.

On to Ontic-Capitalism[55]

We have seen that invention and innovation require both physical and cognitive skills. In view of the phenomenology of Heidegger and Merleau-Ponty we can now say that the two are in fact inseparable. I also argued in this chapter that innovation should be understood in a broader perspective in terms of the development and organization of work and everyday life in society. In other words, creative perception and action, invention and innovation, are essential parts of everyday life, day to day skilful coping with things and people.

Furthermore, I claimed, a *cultural coup* by the masses, who have been robbed of their skills, to claim a *qualitatively* richer world, and an ontologically more satisfying way of life, have become historical necessities with the gradual shift of power to the East. The question is, what kind of new socio-economic organization will emerge, and what will the peoples in the lands of rising sun have to say about it? But perhaps a more pressing question is what sort of a dance we need to dance to the tune of the approaching economic decline in the West, and what you, the reader, has to say about it.

It is, to my mind, highly unlikely that a full Western-style modernism and capitalism could plausibly be established in the

Eurasian landmass. We need to think beyond technological and economic determinism. History does not need to repeat; or maybe it does! As I pointed out in Chapter 2, the first signs of substantial knowledge and capital accumulation emerged around the ninth century in the medieval Islamic world. One would expect capitalism and industrialization would, therefore, emerge in the Western Asia several centuries before Europe; but it didn't. The fact that it didn't is our insurance policy against its future realization in the BRIC (Brazil, Russia, India, China) countries and others. If it didn't happen then, chances are that it may not happen in the future; whether due to the will of the people or other intricate reasons that stem from complex cultural, historical, geographic, climatic and other contingent factors. An alternative post-capitalist re-organization of the East seems inevitable to me.

As for the West, it should be obvious in the wake of the continuing financial crises since 2008, the current model of growth, or what I called the *Vertical Epistemic Development* (VED), cannot be sustained for very long. After the VED what would come to replace it is up for grabs. If turning into a stockpile of brain compost is to be avoided, accumulation of cash has to give way to accumulation of cognitive and manual skills, and integration of 'real' production of things with 'virtual' knowledge production, that is, *Horizontal Ontic Development*, or HOD, as I called it in Chapter 1.

The glorimeters or valuemeters of Tarde may, at the junction of the global swing from VED to HOD, become a viable alternative to the omnipresence of money-based metrics of economic activity. As discussed briefly above, alternative measurements of social rank, status, authority, quality, trustworthiness, and what have you have always been around, but have become particularly conspicuous lately with the advent of the internet and the World Wide Web. The number of friends linking in one's social media pages, number of edits of a Wiki page, number of links to and from a web page, number of comments left in a web log or blog, number of hits a keyword gets in a search engine result list, are some of the ways personal glories and standings are measured on the web today. These sorts of epistemological interests on the web are matched by the intense ontological activity of populating the web with new 'beings' and the relationships between them. This in fact proved to be the most certain way to successful innovation in the brave new cyberworld.

The Web populates the world with documents and the connections or links between them. Web search engines such as Google or Bing exploit the document link structure of the web to measure the value of a page for a given query. Social media applications such as Facebook or LinkedIn populate the world with people, or rather their representations (true or fake), and the relationships between them (genuine or feigned). YouTube populates the cyberworld with multimedia objects, or moving images, sound and music. Applications such as the Amazon Mechanical Turk operate with people who perform tasks which, in Hubert Dreyfus's words, *computers* today *still can't do*. These also happen to be the most popular innovations in the cyber world. Another, groundbreaking and popular application on the internet is Google Earth which provides a detailed model of the earth (also outer space and the depths of the oceans); a prime example of ontologizing the cyber-universe.

And then there are others such as *DrawingNow.com*, a website dedicated to teaching visitors how to draw cartoons: a very useful example to keep in mind in the context of dreaming up of new technologies for skill acquisition and development in antic-ipation of the *onticapitalism* to come.

True, the Web is also full of cheap and saucy commercial activity, spam, adverts, plagiarized texts and other junk, all patrolled and 'mined' by Big Brother for 'intelligence' purposes. If we are to establish a new way of living and working, more of the internet needs to be claimed for establishment of genuine relationships between humans and things, and nurturing and development of new cognitive and artisanal skills. A tall order perhaps, but certainly not out of the reach of our human ingenuity.

Photo courtesy of Cem Devecioğlu.

That's the end of the story folks... hope you enjoyed it.
(Please turn over for *after the end of the end*.)

(For want of an) Afterword

This book aimed to look at innovation and economy from the perspective of the everyday and popular. For one thing, I am a passionate habitué of popular culture, especially, as you no doubt know by now, popular music. To my mind popular music, and in general popular culture, is all about creating collective experiences, pleasures that are 'relevant' to one's own life. For me, there is no higher pleasure than putting oneself in direct contact with the forces that traverse social life on this planet, namely, empathy and creativity, and striving to make do with whatever means are available in the face of the impossibility of evading hegemonic social and economic forces; a struggle which is the mother of all invention. True, popular culture has its dark side too; but let's not spoil the fun for now.

I leave the last word to an artist (well practically to you, the reader, as it is up to you to dig out, or not, his music and lyrics) with whom I had the joy of meeting briefly at a gig that I helped arrange in one early spring day in Ankara... Listening suggestion: *When We Refuse To Suffer*, by Jonathan Richman.

Photo courtesy of Cem Devecioğlu and Seda Usubütün.

End Notes

1   Listening suggestion: *Dedicated to You But You Weren't Listening*, by The Soft Machine.

2   *Human, All Too Human – A Book for Free Spirits*, Friedrich Wilhelm Nietzsche, Cambridge University Press, 1996, para. 376.

3   *Simulacra and Simulation*, Jean Baudrillard, University of Michigan Press, Michigan, 1994.

4   *Understanding Media*, Marshall McLuhan, Routledge, London, 1964.

5   "Brains in a vat", Hilary Putnam. In: Reason, Truth, and History, Chapter 1, pp. 1-21 (Cambridge University Press, 1982).

6   Listening suggestions: *Hearts & Bones*, by Paul Simon; *Why Are We Sleeping*, The Soft Machine.

7   Listening suggestion: *One Trick Pony*, by Paul Simon.

8   Listening suggestion: *Heaven*, by Talking Heads.

9   Since, technically, organic composition is the ratio between constant capital and variable capital, when the contribution of the human element in the production process decreases, it increases. This may suit mathematicians and economists, however, it is counter intuitive! I, therefore, reverse the formula and define it as the ratio between variable capital and constant capital, so that it decreases when the human element in the production process decreases – a more fitting and certainly more intuitive formulation.

10 Listening suggestion: *We have the Technology*, by Pere Ubu.

11 Listening suggestions: *Da Da Da*, by Trio; *Dada Was Here*, The Soft Machine.

12 Attributed to the Prophet Muhammad in the Islamic tradition.

13 Listening suggestion: Anything by Einstürzende Neubauten.

14 *A Country is not a Company*, Paul Krugman, Harvard Business School Press, Boston, Massachusetts, 2009.

15 *Understanding Popular Culture*, John Fiske, Unwin Hyman, Boston, 1989.

16 *The End of Knowing: A New Developmental Way of Learning*, Fred Newman, and Lois Holzman, Routledge, London, 1997.

17 Brier Dudley, 'Bill Gates, Jerry Seinfeld and their churros', *blog.seattletimes*, September 4, 2008. Available from: http://blog.seattletimes.nwsource.com/brierdudley/2008/09/04/bill_gates_jerry_seinfeld_and.html

18 http://www.psu.com/forums/archive/index.php/t-156091.html

19 Daniel Roberts, 'Richard Branson: What Do You Stand For?', *ecademy*, 16 December, 2006. Available from: http://www.ecademy.com/node.php?id=77773

20 Scott Jeffrey, 'The Adventures of Richard Branson', *The "Impossible Journeys" Archive*, October 10, 2003. Available from: http://scottjeffrey.blogspot.co.uk/2002/11/adventures-of-richard-branson.html

21 Anon, 'Virgin Group, Resource: Exploring Corporate Strategy', *Ese Courses Online*. Available from: http://esecourses.com/cfincase.pdf

22 Anon, 'Richard Branson & Virgin, Probably Britain's best known Entrepreneur', *solarnavigator*. Available from: http://www.solarnavigator.net/sponsorship/richard_branson.htm

23 Anon, 'Skills You Need for Business: Introduction to Skills You Need for Business', *Queensland Government Business Development*. Available from: http://skills.business.qld.gov.au/starting/519.htm

24 http://www.microsoft.com/About/Legal/EN/US/Compliance/Buscond/Default.aspx. For a useful analysis of the changes in Microsoft's statements about its values see: http://www.kegel.com/corporate_ethics.html

25 Todd Bishop, 'What Bill Gates and Sam Walton have in common', *Microsoft and Tech News,* March 14, 2006. Available from: http://blog.seattlepi.com/microsoft/2006/03/14/what-bill-gates-and-sam-walton-have-in-common/

26 http://techcrunch.com/2010/02/04/microsoft-civil-wars/

27 John C. Abell, 'Jan. 19, 1983: Apple Gets Graphic With Lisa', *This Day in Tech, Wired,* January 19, 2010. Available from: http://www.wired.com/thisdayintech/2010/01/0119apple-unveils-lisa/

28 *Inside Steve's Brain,* Leander Kahney, Atlantic Books, 2008.

29 Fiachra Gibbons, 'Concept art is pretentious tat, says ICA chief', The Guardian, 17 January 2002. Available from: http://www.guardian.co.uk/uk/2002/jan/17/arts.higheredu-cation

30 *After the End of Art: Contemporary Art and the Pale of History,* Arthur C. Danto, Princeton, Princeton University Press, 1997, p. 112.

31 LeWitt, S. "Paragraphs on conceptual art." In: A. Alberro, & B. Stimson (Eds.), Conceptual art: A critical anthology (2000): (pp. 12-16). Cambridge, Massachusetts: The MIT Press. Original text was published in Artforum, 5:10 (1967): 79-84.

32 *Relational Aesthetics,* Nicolas Bourriaud, Les presses du réel, 2002.

33 In: Robert Lebel: *Marcel Duchamp,* New York, Paragraphic Books, 1959, pp. 77-78.

34 *Information Arts: Intersections of Art, Science and Technology,* Stephen Wilson, MIT Press, 2002.

35 The first three are by artists.

36 For more detailed discussion on this see, "Information Science and Information Arts: Time to Unite?" Murat Karamuftuoglu, Journal of the American Society for Information Science & Technology Volume 57 (13), 2006, pp. 1780-1793.

37 http://billhoss.phpwebhosting.com/ross/index.php?kind

38   *Secret Knowledge – Rediscovering the Lost Techniques of the Old Masters*, David Hockney, Thames & Hudson Ltd, London, 2001.

39   *Felsefenin Işığında Modern Resim* [Modern Painting in Light of Philosophy], İsmail Tunalı, rh+sanat, İstanbul, 1981.

40   *The End of Science: Facing the Limits of Knowledge in the Twilight of the Scientific Age*, John Horgan, Reading, MA, Helix Books/Addison-Wesley Publishing Company, 1996.

41   In: Bennett Simpson, "Public Relations - Nicolas Bourriaud – Interview". Retrieved, from http://www.16beaver group.org/monday/archives/001178.php

42   *The Sciences of the Artificial*, Herbert Alexander Simon, MIT Press, 1996.

43   *Principles of Scientific Management*, Frederick W. Taylor, Harper & Brothers, New York and London, 1911.

44   *The Case for Working with Your Hands, or Why Office Work is Bad for Us and Fixing Things Feels Good*, Matthew Crawford, London, Viking, 2009.

45   "Culture is ordinary", Raymond Williams. In: N. McKenzie (ed.), Convictions, 1958.

46   *21st Century Schizoid Man* is a song by a progressive rock band King Crimson written in the wake of the Vietnam War. Another piece with a similar title and political references is *21st Century Breakdown* released in 2009 by a new generation punk rock band Green Day.

47   Listening suggestion: *The Facts of Life*, by Talking Heads.

48   *How I Learned to Let My Workers Lead*, Ralph Stayer, Harvard Business School Press, Boston, Massachusetts, 2009.

49   Listening suggestion: *Cars*, by Gary Numan.

50   "Self-organization and Clustered control in the Toyota Group: lessons from the Aisin fire", T. Nishiguchi & A. Beaudet. Massachusetts Institute of Technology International Motor Vehicle Program, 1998. Available from: http://dspace .mit.edu/bitstream/handle/1721.1/1457/167a.pdf?sequence=1

51 Steven Spear reported in "How Toyota Turns Workers Into Problem Solvers", Sarah Jane Johnston, November, 2001. Available from: http://hbswk.hbs.edu/item/3512.html

52 *What Computers Still Can't Do: A Critique of Artificial Reason.* Hubert L. Dreyfus, The MIT Press, Cambridge, Mass., 1992.

53 "The Current Relevance of Merleau-Ponty's Phenomenology of Embodiment", Hubert L. Dreyfus. Available from: http://www.focusing.org/apm_papers/dreyfus2.html

54 In: *The Science of Passionate Interests: An Introduction to Gabriel Tarde's Economic Anthropology,* Bruno Latour and Vincent Antonin Lepinay, Prickly Paradigm Press, Chicago, 2009, p. 19.

55 Listening suggestion: *The Bottom Line,* by Big Audio Dynamite.

Contemporary culture has eliminated both the concept of the public and the figure of the intellectual. Former public spaces – both physical and cultural – are now either derelict or colonized by advertising. A cretinous anti-intellectualism presides, cheerled by expensively educated hacks in the pay of multinational corporations who reassure their bored readers that there is no need to rouse themselves from their interpassive stupor. The informal censorship internalized and propagated by the cultural workers of late capitalism generates a banal conformity that the propaganda chiefs of Stalinism could only ever have dreamt of imposing. Zer0 Books knows that another kind of discourse – intellectual without being academic, popular without being populist – is not only possible: it is already flourishing, in the regions beyond the striplit malls of so-called mass media and the neurotically bureaucratic halls of the academy. Zer0 is committed to the idea of publishing as a making public of the intellectual. It is convinced that in the unthinking, blandly consensual culture in which we live, critical and engaged theoretical reflection is more important than ever before.